My Witness
for the Church

BERNARD HÄRING

INTRODUCTION AND TRANSLATION
BY
LEONARD SWIDLER

PAULIST PRESS
New York and Mahwah, N.J.

My Witness for the Church is an English translation of the German edition, *Meine Erfahrung mit der Kirche* (Freiburg: Herder, 1989), which was Häring's own translation of the original Italian interview-based volume, *Fede Storia: Morale Intervista di Gianni Licheri* (Rome, Edizioni Borla, Via delle Fornaci, 50, 1989).

Library of Congress Cataloging-in-Publication Data

Häring, Bernard, 1912–
　　[Fede, storia, morale. English]
　　My witness for the church/Bernard Häring: introduction and translation by Leonard Swidler.
　　　　p.　cm.
　　Translation of: Fede, storia, morale.
　　ISBN 0-8091-3278-8 (pbk.)
　　1. Häring, Bernard, 1912–　—Interviews.　2. Catholic Church
—Clergy—Interviews.　3. Ethicists—Interviews.　4. Christian
ethics—Catholic authors.　5. Catholic Church—Teaching office.
6. Catholic Church—Doctrines.　I. Title
BX4705.H257A5　1992
241'.042'092—dc20
[B]　　　　　　　　　　　　　　　　　　　　　　　　　91-41800
　　　　　　　　　　　　　　　　　　　　　　　　　　　　　CIP

Published by Paulist Press
997 Macarthur Boulevard
Mahwah, N.J. 07430

Printed and bound in the United States of America

CONTENTS

INTRODUCTION: ECCLESIA SEMPER REFORMANDA

Leonard Swidler

Father Bernard Häring has been associated in the minds of numerous Catholics, and others, with the contemporary renewal of moral theology and with the progressive elements of the Second Vatican Council. Many also know him as an eminently pastoral man who has given inspiration, light, and comfort to Catholic and non-Catholic alike. He is also known as a man of uncommon courage who has faced death many times in war—having led his fellow German soldiers, unarmed, out of the death-ring of Stalingrad—and in the past dozen years having successfully fought a deadly battle of many operations with cancer of the throat.

Now we learn that all these qualities were being mightily tested, and strengthened, in the fire of a constant struggle against the secret, and not so secret, forces of repression within the high reaches of the Catholic Church. This is a moving, and inspiring, witness to Bernard Häring's suffering love for the Catholic Church and every man and woman within and without it that is indeed an *Imitatio Christi* from which every Catholic, and others as well, should take courage.

Early in 1989 Father Häring published much of this unknown story in a book, first in Italian,[1] which was bluntly critical of many of the present practices in the Church and called for a series of progressive reforms. Already by the beginning of 1990 it had gone through six printings of the German edition and had been translated into Spanish and French. Moreover, Häring wrote me a few months ago that he had already had over a thousand supporting letters in response to his book—a clear sign of grassroots yearning for progressive renewal and reform. In translating this book at times I have gasped in shock, cried in sorrow—and in the end shouted: Hurrah!

Although Häring's witness really needs no introduction, perhaps for those who have not consistently followed the happy/unhappy Catholic news of recent years—or suppressed it—the following recollections, reflections, and at the end, concrete suggestions, will provide a setting, particularly of American Catholicism, within which to hear Häring's witness.

1. *Vatican II Mandate for Church Renewal*

"Christ summons the Church, as she goes her pilgrim way, to that *continual reformation of which she always has need.*" [Emphasis mine] Not the words of Martin Luther, John Calvin or some other sixteenth-century Reformer, but those of all the Catholic bishops of the world, including the pope, at the Second Vatican Council.

---

[1] Bernard Häring, *Fede Storia Morale Intervista di Gianni Licheri* (Rome: Borla, 1989). The German translation, done by Häring himself, is entitled: *Meine Erfahrung mit der Kirche* (Freiburg: Herder, 1989).

Indeed, the pope and bishops were even more insistent when they said: "All are led . . . wherever necessary, to undertake with vigor the task of renewal and reform." The pope and bishops did not say all bishops, nor even all priests or all religious, but simply, "all," that is, all those to whom that *Decree on Ecumenism* was addressed, namely, all the Catholic faithful.

Moreover, this mandate to renewal and reform was not conceived as a luxury for those Catholics who have nothing else to do. Rather, it is a duty that is incumbent on *all* Catholics, as the pope and bishops made clear: "Catholics' . . . primary duty is to make a careful and honest appraisal of whatever needs to be renewed and done in the Catholic household."[2]

2. *Vatican II Implementation*

Many in the Catholic laity, religious, clergy and even hierarchy—depending on which pope appointed the bishop—responded positively to the charge to renew and reform the Church to make it relevant to today's world (*aggiornamento* in Pope John XXIII's word). Renewal moved ahead with great elan for the first few years after the end of the Council in 1965. However, it received what many perceive as its first major setback in 1968, with Pope Paul VI's encyclical on birth control, *Humanae vitae*.

Another negative blow came when the recommendation to change the electors of the pope from the papal-appointed cardinals to delegates elected by the national bishops' conferences around the world did not receive the expected approval—even though its draft had been re-

---

[2] All three citations are from the Vatican II *Decree on Ecumenism*, sections 4 and 5.

quested by the pope. This decree sat on Pope Paul's desk already in 1970, but he was dissuaded from signing it by conservative Curial elements.

Had he made this momentous decision, the subsequent history of Catholic Church renewal might well have been radically different. Every new pope would necessarily have had a sense of responsibility to, and more collegiality with, his "constituents," the representatives of the world Church. But most importantly, this structural change at the top would have released an irresistible movement for bishops to be "elected" in some meaningful way by their "constituents," and then also the pastors in turn.

As the Church moved further into the 1970s it seems that Pope Paul became less decisive, wanting on the one hand to carry out the Vatican II mandate of renewal and reform, while on the other fearing the specter of error and anarchy that was constantly whispered in his ear. Then came Pope Paul's death in 1978 and his replacement first by the briefly reigning (one month) Paul John I, and then the long-reigning John Paul II.

3. *1979—A Year of Retrenchment*

I believe 1979 was a bad year for renewal and reform. 1) Already in the spring of 1979 the French theologian Jacques Pohier was silenced for his book *When I Speak of God.* 2) In July a team of four American theologians, appointed by the Catholic Theological Society of America, found their sexuality book (which had been accepted by the CTSA) condemned. 3) In September the Jesuit General in Rome Father Pedro Arrupe was forced to send a letter to all Jesuits warning them that they could not publicly dissent from any papal position. 4) All autumn severe accusations of heresy against Edward Schillebeeckx were issued recurrently in the press; December 13–15 Schille-beeckx was "interrogated" by the Holy Office in Rome. 5) That same month writings of Brazilian liberation theologian Leonardo Boff were "condemned" (he was later silenced for a year). 6) Then on December 18—at exactly the same time Pope John Paul II said, "Truth is the power of peace. . . . What should one say of the practice of combatting or silencing those who do not share the same views?"[3]—the Holy Office issued a Declaration on Hans Küng saying he "can no longer be considered a Catholic theologian."

The response to the condemnation of Hans Küng was vocal, extensive and largely negative, not only around the Catholic world, but the "ecumenical" world as well. Küng himself received over five thousand letters of support. The next months were agonizing ones for Catholics, but in the end a "compromise" was reached for Professor Küng at the Catholic Theology Faculty of the University of Tübingen where he teaches: Küng would no longer be a member of the Catholic Faculty, but would retain his chair of Ecumenical Theology and his directorship of the Ecumenical Institute; he would also retain the right to put forward doctoral candidates in the Catholic Theology Faculty (there never was any official question but that he remained a priest in good standing—to this very day).

Still, the result was that Küng no longer has the influence within official Catholic ecclesiastical circles he had before 1979. On the other hand, his general popularity and influence seems to have increased. Whereas up to 1979 he would normally have 150 students attending his lecture courses at the University of Tübingen, now every year when he lectures between 1,000 and 2,000 attend.

---

[3] Reported in the *Washington Post*, December 19, 1979.

One further interesting result of the Küng affair is that three Catholic Rights groups were founded: "Christenrechte in der Kirche" (Germany), "Droits et libertes dans les Eglise" (France) and the "Association for the Rights of Catholics in the Church"—ARCC (United States)—all of which are still active. These are organizations that understand themselves to be making a contribution to the Church and world in the area of the rights of Catholics in the Church in keeping with the urging of the 1971 International Synod of Bishops when it declared that "within the Church rights must be preserved. No one should be deprived of his ordinary rights because he is associated with the Church"; and with the subsequent Canon 208 of the 1983 Code of Canon Law, when it stated that "there exists among all the Christian faithful, a true equality."

One of the first tasks ARCC undertook was to draft a *Charter of the Rights of Catholics in the Church*, which after a great deal of work and world-wide consultation was first issued in 1983. In 1988 a commentary on the *Charter* was published in the book *A Catholic Bill of Rights*, and a German version appeared in September, 1990.

4. *Contemporary American Catholicism*

Many American Catholics have experienced the dozen subsequent years of the pontificate of Pope John Paul II as a combination of his charismatic promotion of human rights and social justice in the secular sphere, matched by a tendency toward authoritarianism and centralization within the Church—thereby projecting in the world a credibility-damaging image of a potential double-standard.

Whether one accepts this interpretation or not, it is

very interesting to look at the profile of American Catholicism as it was drawn by an extensive scientific poll just before Pope John Paul II's visit to the U.S. in September of 1987. Sunday church attendance dropped from a pre-*Humanae vitae* (1968) 65% to 50% in 1975, but has remained steady ever since. Before Vatican II American Catholics were characterized by a stress on doctrinal orthodoxy, ritual regularity and obedience to clerical authorities.[4]

That docility has dramatically diminished. Now 70% of American Catholics surveyed think a person can be a good Catholic and not necessarily go to church every Sunday. In another survey 79% opposed the Vatican prohibition on artificial birth control; 73% believed divorced Catholics should remain in the Church; 58% were in favor of married priests and 60% of women priests (statistics consistently show that every time the Vatican publicly condemned the idea of women priests the percentage of support for it rises, starting with 29% at the time of the Vatican Declaration against women priests in 1977[5] to the most recent figure of 60% in favor); 90% said that a person could dissent from Church doctrine and remain a good Catholic; and only 26% believed in papal infallibility.

But American Catholics have not abandoned the Church in large numbers, as the drop in docility might suggest would happen. Rather, they are staying in. As sociologist Teresa A. Sullivan says, "There is something American Catholics find in Catholicism that is deep and nurturing and doesn't have very much to do with the Vatican and

---

4 See Gerhard Lenski, "The Religious Factor, 1961," referred to in "NCR Gallup Poll," *National Catholic Reporter*, September 11, 1987, p. 10.

5 Cf. Leonard Swidler, "Roma Locuta, Causa Finita?" in: Leonard Swidler and Arlene Swidler, eds., *Women Priests A Catholic Commentary on the Vatican Declaration* (New York: Paulist, 1977), p. 3.

the bishops and all the rest."[6] At the same time, sociologist Ruth A. Wallace notes that the Gallup survey finds among American Catholics an "eagerness with which the laity seem to want to participate in a lot of policy questions, no matter what age or level of education."[7] The survey further strengthens what Joseph Fichter, S.J. found a decade earlier:

> The church is being modernized in spite of itself. It appears that the changes are occurring at the bottom of the structure. American Catholicism is experiencing adaptation at the grass roots. The most significant aspect of this change is the switch of emphasis in the basis of moral and religious guidance. Dependence on legislation from above has largely switched to dependence on the conscience of the people.[8]

Even more interesting in the Gallup survey figures are those reflecting the attitudes of the large bulge in the American population, the so-called "baby-boomers," those born between 1948 and 1957. They represent not only a disproportionately large segment of the American population, because the Catholic "baby-boom" was even larger than the America boom in general, but they are really the trend-setters for the future of the American Catholic Church. And they seem to be more liberal than the average Catholic, more pro-democracy, pro-reform in the Church. The same is also true of educated Catholics:

---

[6] "NCR Gallup Poll," p. 10.

[7] Ibid.

[8] Joseph H. Fichter, "Restructuring Catholicism: Symposium on Thomas O'Dea," *Sociological Analysis*, 38 (1977), pp. 163f.

the more educated the Catholics, the greater the likelihood of their being liberal, pro-renewal and reform, arguably more mature—and American Catholics are rapidly becoming increasingly more educated.

One of the most recent signs of a rising American Catholic grass-roots movement for renewal and reform in the Church is the "Call for Reform in the Catholic Church —A Pastoral Letter from 4505 Catholics Concerned about Fundamental Renewal of our Church," which appeared in the February 28, 1990 *New York Times*. The sponsors, including ARCC, were hoping, in the end, to gather 100,000 signatures.

This is no wild radical rebellion, but a moderate call for reform that reiterates the call for several of the basic reforms repeated by a wide range of Catholic individuals and groups, including the "Charter of Rights of Catholics in the Church" issued by ARCC. The "Call" grounded its concerns as follows:

> The Church should be providing wisdom and encouragement to believers to enter the dialogue on these issues [poverty, environment, peace, etc.]. Unfortunately, today's Church is crippled by its failure to address fundamental justice issues within its own institutional structures. It thus becomes a stumbling block both to its own members and to society.
>
> We therefore appeal to the institutional church to reform and renew its structures.

This call for reform of structures includes most importantly 1) "Incorporating women at all levels of ministry and decision-making"; 2) "opening the priesthood to women and married men, including resigned priests"; 3) lay, religious and clergy participation "in the selection of our local bishops, a time-honored tradition in the church"; 4) "open dialogue [with theologians], academic freedom, and due process"; 5) "a process that allows all those affected to be heard from, and to take part in these decisions."

From all evidence, these seem to be practical, basic reforms that the majority of American Catholics support. In short, while American Catholics are staying in the Church in droves, they are yearning for both an inward and outward renewal in the letter and spirit of Vatican II—precisely the sort Father Häring exemplifies and passionately calls for in this book.

1

CHILDHOOD AND CHOICE
OF VOCATION

Time and again in your writings you express your grati-
tude for your homelife. Could you say something in more
detail? [All questions are by Dr. Gianni Licheri.]

I was born on November 10, 1912, the eleventh of
twelve children. I was clearly a desired and welcomed
child. I grew up under the sun of my family's love. Two of
my twelve siblings died in childhood. The remaining ten of
us got along well together and were proud of each other
—as we still are today. My father was a successful farmer
who was proud of his class. The farm was my mother's
inheritance. My grandfather on my father's side was a
brewer and innkeeper. I knew my grandparents only from
hearing about them.

My mother was an excellent housewife and, more importantly, a wise educator. My father loved and respected
her deeply. Their marriage was a model of what today is
called a partnership marriage. Even today, after all my
experiences I could not imagine a more ideal set of parents. My mother was extraordinarily hospitable. If a beg-
gar knocked on the door before midday meal—and this

often happened—he would hear, "Today you will be our guest." In those times we were relatively well off. If poverty befell a family with many children, this did not go unnoticed by my mother. She helped as long as it was necessary. It was a daily privilege for us children to bring infirm or elderly people to our midday meal. My mother embodied nonviolence in model fashion. I can never remember her shouting at one of the children or hitting them in irritation.

My father was by nature short-tempered, but under the influence of his wife he also became increasingly gentle. My two older brothers told us that one time my father severely punished them in anger. But mother then said to him: "Johannes, your hand is too heavy. Leave the punishment to me, if any is needed." He accepted this as if it were a command from God. My father was also outspokenly altruistic. He would often spend Sunday afternoon writing letters for neighbors who could not manage such things.

Our parents' faith was the air we breathed. According to my great-aunt (the grandmother of the later Federal Chancellor Kurt Georg Kiesinger), even as a young man my father was a weekly communicant. During my childhood he went to communion daily, often after he had already worked for several hours. My mother was no less devout, but of course housework and caring for us children did not allow her to attend daily Mass. She blessed each of us children with holy water in the morning and in the evening. My parents' devotion was a healthy one, without a breath of sentimental piety.

Almost every day in winter friends and neighbors came to visit us, spending the long evenings in our large sitting room. We prayed the rosary together with the guests and often my mother also read a page from the Holy

Scriptures or from the life of a saint. If the men told stories about ghosts or other superstitious things my mother chided them humorously: "You just never learn!" She was brilliant in knowing how to turn the discussion away from these things.

What effect did the political situation, World War I, post-war poverty and National Socialism have in your parents' house?

My otherwise happy childhood was painfully disturbed by the events of the First World War. My oldest brother served three years on the Western Front. My second-oldest brother volunteered before reaching the age of mandatory service in order to keep my father free from military service. I can still remember how vigorously my father protested against this step, but my brother was in earnest. He simply could not believe that a father of small children should be required to do war service.

Toward the end of the war my oldest brother had a furlough. He told my parents that he would not return to the front, but would hide himself in my parents' house or somewhere else until the war was over. My father and the local pastor, however, convinced him to return to his post. When he was once again at the front he wrote that he was sorry to have caused his father this vexation, and that incidentally he would soon meet his younger brother since their regiments had been stationed alongside one another.

Just as the war ended two announcements of "missing in action," one for each brother, arrived at our home on the same day. The letter carrier knew that my mother was sick at the time and so brought the two letters to a relative, trusting that she would carefully break the news to my parents. It is still very clear in my memory how our father made us swear not to cry or to go into mother's sickroom with red eyes. Nevertheless, our mother, who was very ill, saw it on our faces and asked: "Which of the two is fallen?" When no answer came, she answered herself: "Both of them!" In fact it was only the oldest one who had fallen. After months we learned that the other brother was being held as a prisoner of war by the English. He came home ill, and suffered from lupus, which he had contracted while a prisoner. This depressed my father severely since Wenzel had volunteered in order to spare him military service. My father spared neither effort nor money to get him the help of the best physicians.

My father was politically very involved. Throughout all these years he was the local chairman of the Center Party. The task of carrying about its promotional material fell to us children.

Since there was a great deal of unemployment in our area it is understandable that the Communist Party gained many voters. Even as a young student I read the works of Karl Marx, partly in order to be able to stand up in communist gatherings as a counter-speaker. Although I never felt inclined toward Marxism, nevertheless, through reading Marx and Engels I learned to resist every attempt to subordinate religion to the purposes of the rich and powerful.

When the great landowner Freiherr von Papen, the Center Party man who presented himself as very Catholic, brought down the government of Brüning (Center-Social Democrats) in protest against a planned land reform (1932), I wrote a dramatic play entitled "The Social Deed." The content was:

> First Act: There was a great landowner who had squandered the generous public subsidies in the city for his own benefit and had exploited his

many farmworkers. Then, his eyes were opened. He confessed his sins in front of his workers, asked for forgiveness and for the privilege of being allowed to work as one of them on the land. He received their consent.

Second Act: The other great landowners took counsel how they could punish this traitor if he did not return to solidarity with his class.

Third Act: They berated him and killed him. But at this moment a messenger announced: "Just now the Red Army has moved into Königsberg."

Ironically, thirteen years later, as a soldier of a defeated army and then as a prisoner of war, I saw the East Prussian Junkers in despairing flight before the Red Army, carrying what they could of their possessions.

When Hitler came to power in 1933 he distributed free radios to every family. My father firmly declared: "As long as this criminal screams on the radio, there will be no radio in my house!" And several years later when Hitler honored mothers of many children with the "Mother's Cross," my mother was to receive a golden one. She declined to go to receive the honor. When a Party functionary came to the house to deliver the honor, she politely opened the door and said: "I will not accept this honor because I have not borne and raised any of my children for National Socialism!"

In 1934, a large military practice area for the SS was planned within the limits of our community. Many farmers, thinking of the prospect of a very large compensatory payment, were prepared to cede parcels of land. My father went from house to house and simply asked the question: "Have you also thought about your daughters?"

That struck home with all of them. At the decisive assembly the farmers unanimously rejected the voluntary handing over of their land. At that time I was in the novitiate of the Redemptorists. My father wrote to me: "You will probably not receive a letter from me for quite some time because an extended retreat in the Heuberg lies before me." Among us Heuberg meant: "Concentration camp."

In a climate like this, how did you come to a vocation in the religious life?

I was a rather lazy student in primary school for I was much more interested in our horses than in homework. Nevertheless, at age twelve I made up my mind to study so that perhaps one day I could become a missionary. I completed my diploma in March of 1933 at the state Gymnasium in Günzburg. Since I was the first in the class I had to deliver the valedictory address. I spoke of the hard wanderings in the desert which lay before us in the coming years, for which we needed courage and hope. Those professors of mine who had been tainted by National Socialism resented my speech, but many others, including my schoolmates, welcomed it.

Now I had to make a decision concerning my vocation. I admit openly that it was not easy for me to give up marriage and a family. However, the conviction that the world had no more pressing need than proclaimers of the Gospel was decisive for me. Since I had a great admiration for the missionaries of the Society of Jesus, like Matteo Ricci and Francis Xavier, I inquired about the Jesuit order in Germany. However, when I learned that they had two different training tracks, one for the gifted who would become professors, I eliminated this alternative. In no case did I want to become a bookworm or professor. Then, after the Provincial Superior of the South German Redemptorists assured me that with them I need not fear becoming a professor, I decided to join them. After my profession he repeated this assurance and advised me to learn the language and culture of Brazil since members of the Province would constantly be sent there. He asked me in a friendly manner not to speak of this until I had my ship's passage; otherwise the professors could cross up my plans. I followed his advice in every regard.

How did your family look upon your choice of vocation?

My parents were happy about it. However, they had never attempted to persuade me to make this choice. At the time of my entrance into the novitiate, when my father brought me to the train station in his landauer, he cautiously asked me: "Why are you going so far away? Could you not become a diocesan priest?" My answer basically was: "I do not feel like a hero. I need the support and encouragement of a community." This made a lot of sense to him. Nevertheless he added: "Whatever you decide is right with us. If you return to us, you are also welcome. And if you should again take up your earlier plan about studying medicine, we will be helpful in that as well."

How did you experience the Hitler years in your religious order?

Of the ten of us novices, there was only one who expected something good from Hitler's government. The rest of us were not surprised that our superiors very soon sent that young man away, being convinced that he lacked the necessary gift of discernment. I can still remember quite well how Cardinal Faulhaber, while on a visit with us in Gars, where he always felt at home, once said: "The National Socialism of Hitler is not only a heresy, but the sum of all heresies."

When Hitler marched into Austria, anger, fury and finally deep depression pervaded all of us in Gars, which was not far from the Austrian border. But nobody spoke very publicly about it. When we learned of the cowardly behavior of the Austrian bishops we were very disturbed, until we heard about the miserable extortion of Goebbels.

The position in our house and in our province was unanimous. Hence, when Bishop Sproll had to flee my home diocese of Rottenburg because of the SS, we could provide him a temporary secure hiding place in Gars. Likewise Professor Steinbüchl, who later became my Doctor-Father, found a secure place with us and felt very much at home.

During your study time at Gars did you already feel an inclination toward moral theology?

Quite the contrary. I had once read a sentence by Paul Claudel: "Certainly, we love Christ; but nothing in the world can move us to like moralism." I found my own feelings classically expressed in this sentence. I studied history, philosophy, sociology, dogma and above all exegesis with enthusiasm. I felt very disinclined toward moral theology, as it was taught at that time, and also canon law.

Ultimately, however, I discovered that moral theology also could be different. I read the books of Johann Michael Sailer, Johann Baptist Hirscher, and also the moral theology of Fritz Tillmann. Finally, I discovered the ethics of value of Max Scheler and Dietrich von Hildenbrand. I could become enthusiastic about these, but never in my wildest dream did I think that one day I might teach moral theology.

Thus, my surprise was all the greater when, shortly after my ordination to the priesthood, as I was preparing for my departure to Brazil, my provincial superior disclosed to me that the college of professors absolutely needed a professor of moral theology at that time. I told my superior that this was my very last choice because I found the teaching of moral theology an absolute crashing bore. He mollified me with the answer: "We are asking you to prepare yourself for this task with a doctorate from a German university precisely so that it can be different in the future."

In obedience I said yes, although it was difficult for me. This downpayment in trust gave me courage and no doubt was a rich capital resource for the rest of my life. I decided to go to Tübingen to take my doctorate there, especially in view of the historically oriented tradition of that theological school. Soon after I discussed the matter with Professor Steinbüchl, who at that time was a hidden guest with us. He suggested to me what he described as the great theme of the century: "The holy and the good— the mutual relationship between religion and morality." He also indicated that in the school of Edmund Husserl and with Max Scheler and others I could doubtless find adequate stimulation for my topic.

2

THE WAR

In your book War Memoirs *you reflected on your war experiences and wrote a kind of narrative theology. What significance did these experiences have for your development as a theologian?*

I was among the first group of priests who were called up for war service. According to the Concordat we could opt for medical service. After my basic training in the fall of 1939 it was possible for my superior to arrange an extended furlough for me through his personal connections with a General Staff physician. Thus, I taught moral theology in our order's theology faculty at Gars from January to July 1940. Already at that time I worked on a plan for my book which later appeared as *The Law of Christ*. I was absolutely determined not to lose myself in problems which were distant from life while the world was in flames.

Then in September 1940, as I registered at the theological faculty in Tübingen to begin my doctoral studies, I was again called up. I was assigned to a medical company stationed in France. The company commander and company sergeant were well-disposed toward me. Thus I could also be active in pastoral work without disturbance. Every Sunday I celebrated Holy Mass and could also preach. Almost the entire company as well as soldiers from the neighboring units participated regularly. After a couple of weeks I began to celebrate Sunday liturgy in the cathedral of Bayeux for the division stationed there. At that time I travelled about on a bicycle until the city commandant, a general, stopped me. I presumed he was going to chew me out about what right I had to celebrate the liturgy, for I knew well that every kind of pastoral work was forbidden to us priests in the medical service, under the threat of several years of imprisonment. But the general approached me in a friendly manner and asked whether it would be all right if he were to order the regimental band to provide music for the religious service. In addition, he arranged to have me picked up by car and brought to the services at the cathedral. I am sure that the general knew just as well as I that my pastoral activity was "contrary to the law." Time and again I had the good fortune of meeting such commanders.

Since I spoke French I was assigned by my company to a number of tasks which brought me into contact with the local population. For the French Catholics I was a priest, and as such it was obvious for them that I was not to be numbered among the "occupying forces." In fact, a number of warm friendships with some families and even some French priests developed.

In the beginning of May 1941, our division was redeployed to Poland on the Russian border. Again I was the contact man with the civilian population. Among other things, I was assigned as a troop medical corpsman for an infantry battalion. I did not know whether the commander had a positive attitude toward the Church or not, but nevertheless I immediately began to hold Bible hours and religious services for interested soldiers, Catholic and Protestant. Soon many Poles also came to my religious services, for the liturgical language of that time was still Latin. The adjutant, who was not well-disposed toward me, complained about this. I had to appear before the commander wearing my steel helmet and combat uniform. He asked me whether it was true that I had held religious services for Poles. I answered that this had in fact occurred a number of times. To his curt question of whether I had anything else to say in my defense, I answered with a request, namely, that my case be judged along with the adjutant who on a number of occasions had drunk and danced with Polish girls. The colonel looked angrily at the officer in question and then sent me away unmolested.

Thus I learned to live with risk. This was often very necessary for me later when I became more and more known as a theologian. I learned to overcome fear. Fear has always been a stimulus for me to stand up courageously in the Church for my convictions.

Then the senseless war against Russia began. On the night before its outbreak, we were informed that the battle was about to begin. I celebrated the liturgy with general absolution and communion for all, Catholic and Protestant. Almost all the soldiers of the unit participated. I cared for the wounded and dying both as a medic and as a priest, regardless of whether they were Orthodox, Protestant or Catholic. I baptized the children of the Orthodox wherever I was asked to. And it happened ever increasingly. Since I also looked after the sick and wounded among the local population, it was soon also known everywhere that I was a priest. I spoke Ukrainian and Russian poorly, but still celebrated baptism in Russian. Thus I grew step by step into my ecumenical vocation, which for me as a theologian has been absolutely decisive.

I experienced in my own body that there are good people everywhere. My battle comrades not only came to religious services and for spiritual counselling, but many times they helped me, with no small risk to themselves, to free Russian prisoners of war, especially when it concerned wounded who had recovered. With a still greater risk they twice helped me to save the lives of many Jews, especially Jewish women.

And I also experienced the goodness of the Russian people in a gripping manner. As we broke out of the ring around Stalingrad—without weapons—Russian peasants gave me their sleighs and horses so I could take a substantial number of wounded with me. Without the kindness of the Russian populace at that time we would have starved and frozen to death—and had we survived, we would have been taken prisoner. When at the capitulation of our armies I did become a Russian prisoner of war, courageous Poles freed me from prison and without any higher approval made me their pastor.

I could go on much longer relating all the kindnesses that I experienced from people of other nations who had been trampled upon by my nation. Is it not of absolutely decisive significance for a moral and pastoral theologian to believe in the goodness of humankind? And it is precisely that which I learned time and again during the war. I learned to trust in Divine Providence, again manifoldly mediated through good people. My return from the East was possible only through an entire chain of extraordinary acts of human goodness. Thus I experienced together the goodness of human beings and the working of Divine Providence. That was decisive for my vocation as a moral theologian.

Unfortunately I also experienced the most absurd obedience by Christians—God have mercy—toward a criminal regime. And that too radically affected my thinking and acting as a moral theologian. After the war I re-

turned to moral theology with the firm decision to teach it
so that its core concept would not be obedience but responsibility, the courage to be responsible. I believe I
have remained true to this decision—of course not to the
damage to genuine obedience, that is, to an obedience
that is responsible and joined to openness and a critical sense.

*What would you now view as the most significant thing
for your vocation which you took away with you from this
absurd war?*

The experiences of the war, the intimate experience
of senseless killing and dying, the personal witnessing of
the brutalizing of many, have made me into a sworn enemy of war. I find it absolutely laughable and at the same
time frustrating that at my age I still have to pour out so
much energy on questions like flexibility or inflexibility
concerning the forbidding of contraception and in the
struggle against sexual rigorism. I am most deeply convinced that my main calling is and must be that of an untiring peace apostle for the elimination of war, for a world
culture that is free of violence, for a radical love that will
not allow us to become enemies, for a "transformation of
armament" to a nonviolent defense. That is the most important thing that has been written onto my conscience as
a result of my war experiences.

*Did you know about the death camps of National So-
cialism when you returned from the East?*

I did not yet know the entire truth, but I still knew
quite a lot. I knew very well about the mass annihilation of
Jews first in Kiev and then in Kharkov. In the night before

the mass shooting of Jews in Kharkov, my best friend and I went on foot to Jews wherever we could find them to warn them not to obey the order for "resettlement"; rather, they should go underground. I learned to be ashamed of myself as a Christian, that even Christians and Church authorities had in many ways been guilty of antisemitism.

From the knowledge of the death camps it was also clear to me how important and at the same time how difficult reconciliation and the healing of such deep historically guiltladen wounds would be. But precisely for these reasons a love that overcomes enmity, a reconciliation as well as nonviolence, must be a special fundamental goal of Catholic moral theology.

3

FROM THE END OF THE WAR
TO VATICAN II

*What were your plans after your return from Poland in
late autumn 1945?*

Strictly speaking, I really had no plans. On the one
hand I realized that there was very much to do and to
change in moral theology. On the other hand I was at-
tracted by practical pastoral work, for which the war years
and the half year in a Polish parish were a good preparation. I presented myself to the Redemptorists in Stuttgart
even before I went home. To begin with, I needed a valid
German identity card for the French occupation zone, in
which my home town lay. Until then I possessed only my
Polish identity card. I let my provincial superior know that
I was alive and at the same time expressed my supposition
that in the meanwhile an alternate professor of moral theology doubtless had been found. I likewise requested permission to immediately take over a number of mission sta-
tions in parishes. With the approval of the superior I
received a mission a short time later. Nevertheless, a letter
from the rector of the monastery and theology faculty in

Gars arrived with the pressing request that I immediately look for a room in Tübingen so that I could finish my doctorate under the direction of Professor Steinbüchl as quickly as possible.

I presumed—correctly—that the professors in Gars were not successful in convincing the provincial superior to order me directly to finish my doctoral studies and to teach moral theology. Thus I went with specific thoughts in the back of my head to Tübingen: first I asked an old cousin of mine whether one of her three student rooms were still free. Wringing her hands, she declared that there were two students lodged in every room. I cheerfully searched further, seeking out the nuns with whom I had earlier found lodging. They also made it clear to me that in Tübingen, the main headquarters of the French occupying forces, there were no rooms available. After careful reflection I now turned my steps to a pastor whom I knew well and asked him to testify for me that it was impossible for a priest to find living quarters in Tübingen at this time. To my surprise, however, he told me that on that very day two upright women had been to him and told him that each one gladly would make available a room for a priest studying for a doctorate. So I bit the sour apple, convinced that somehow Divine Providence so willed it.

As my first-semester lecture I chose to attend one by Professor Karl Adam. After the lecture he waited for me, greeted me most warmly, and then admonished me not to lose any of my precious time. Instead of attending his lectures, he suggested I should work on my dissertation. During the following two semesters I attended the lectures of Romano Guardini and of Theodor Steinbüchl and also those of three of the most highly respected Protestant professors: Körbele, Thielicke and Rückert. I was firmly determined to solidify my ecumenical calling.

Did your doctoral dissertation also have this ecumenical dimension?

My doctoral dissertation, completed in 1947 and published in 1950, was a work which consciously employed ecumenical thought. I analyzed the mutual influence between faith and morality, religion and custom, in the thought of six significant thinkers: Max Scheler in his Catholic period, the Protestant philosopher Immanuel Kant, the consciously and decisively atheistic phenomenologist and value ethicist Nicolai Hartmann, as well as three significant Protestant theologians, namely, Friedrich Schleiermacher, Rudolf Otto, Emil Brunner— and all of this with a completely non-apologetic method. The question is no longer: "How can we defend ourselves?" but rather: "What can we learn from each other and with each other?" The book received ecumenical attention. Soon after its appearance the University of Göttingen requested permission to publish it in Braille. The book was translated into a number of languages.

What was your activity after your doctoral graduation?

In 1947 I took up my teaching responsibility as Professor of Moral Theology and Moral Philosophy at the religious theological faculty at Gars am Inn. Soon thereafter, however, I also added lectures in family and religious sociology. But my pastoral interest permeated more than my teaching activity. Until 1953 I spent my holidays, which lasted about ten weeks, providing pastoral help for the Catholic refugees who found themselves in pressing circumstances in the previously Protestant areas. Along with a courageous home missionary, and with my colleague and

teacher Viktor Schurr, we undertook a new pastoral experiment, the so-called "Refugees' Mission," in areas in
which as yet no Catholic pastoral work had been organized, such as Coburg in northern Bavaria. We wandered
from place to place and visited all families, who often were
living in miserable quarters. We shared their poverty,
slept with the poorest, often together in a single tiny
room. We preached the Good News in rented dance halls
whenever we did not have the good fortune to be invited
by Protestant pastors into their churches.

Before this experiment I had carefully worked out fifteen sermon outlines. Not one of them was ever used.
After the first home visit it became clear to me that it was
not I who should be determining the topics. What should
happen was that I ought to respond to the real life problems, fears, hopes and needs of these men and women.
Again and again I learned a responsorial pastoral work
went hand in hand with a responsorial moral theology.

How did your world-famous moral theological work
The Law of Christ *come about?*

From the first day it was clear to me that in such a time
of massive transformations one could not simply turn back
to earlier written textbooks. My experiences as a wander-
ing preacher for the refugees increasingly strengthened
this insight. Hence, for my lectures I carefully worked out
a new text. At first I did not think about publication. The
stimulation came from my students—most of them were
returned prisoners of war—and from the publisher of my
book *The Holy and the Good*, Dr. Erich Wewel, a student
of Steinbüchl.

Steinbüchl himself, who had prophesied a successful
writing future for me, had asked me to offer my first book,

and whenever possible, further ones, to this sympathetic and completely capable publisher "to help him get back on his feet." Before the Nazi period Wewel had built up a small publishing house, and in doing so proved himself extraordinarily capable. Thus it came about that the Nazi publication house Eher offered him a high post. Dr. Wewel indignantly rejected this offer, but he had to pay dearly for his convictions. His own publishing house was completely destroyed and he had to go to prison for an extended time. After the war, with borrowed money he started anew. In 1953, as I completed my manuscript *The Law of Christ*, Wewel wanted it without question, but told me frankly that he must first of all arrange for a loan. I was prepared to wait.

In 1954 the work appeared in a single thick volume. The prize of "The Most Beautiful Book of the Year" was awarded it by the Society of German Booksellers. Dr. Wewel had poured all of his care and competence into this book. Within a year it went through three printings. The publishing house stood on firm footing. In a few years the work also appeared in fourteen foreign languages, including Japanese and Chinese. The future Cardinal Garonne wrote a glowing foreword for the French edition, which appeared in 1955.

How did it happen that you were called to Rome so early?

The newly elected Superior General of the Redemptorist Order, Leonard Buijs, who previously had been Professor of Moral Theology at Wittem in Holland, got in touch with me immediately after I finished my doctorate. He spoke with me about his plans to help overcome an ancient error in Catholic moral theology. For a long time the religious superiors and bishops had sent all of their prospective professors of moral theology to study canon law or both canon law and civil law in Rome. That served to confirm institutionally the legalism of Catholic moral theology. He envisioned a theology faculty which would specialize in moral theology in its complete thematic breadth and theological-philosophical depth in order to train authentic moral theologians and to prepare them for their real task. He wished to begin on an experimental basis as quickly as possible, starting with a program mainly for Redemptorists. He placed great stock in getting a professor from the Tübingen school—and for this he had his eye on me. In 1948 he asked me to come for a semester to Rome in order to strategize with him and several others. He also thought that it could be useful for me and for his plan if I would look into the teaching procedures of the different Roman faculties.

Have any "Roman experiences" from this time remained more vividly than others in your memory?

Yes, I would like to mention three things. I attended several lectures by the Jesuit Franz Xaver Hürth, who, along with his confrere P. A. Vermeersch, was known as the main editor of the encyclical *Casti connubii*. Father Hürth had many listeners. A gigantic lecture hall was usually filled. He spoke fluent Latin and his lectures were good. But the content was something else again. For example, he spent an entire period on the "important question" of whether a priest in the diaspora should be allowed to celebrate Mass twice on a weekday if this was the only way it would be possible for a number of Catholics to attend Mass at least once a year. I can still see him before me with his dramatic gestures and conclusion: "the answer can

only be a negative one. For there has never and nowhere
been a law to attend Mass on a weekday. Hence, there is
no basis for bination (the celebration of two Masses) on a
weekday by the same priest."

I awaited a storm of indignation. However, nothing of
the sort happened. The listeners openly swore by the
word of the famous teacher, a pillar of the Holy Office. I
took my hat and departed, deeply shaken: So, the Eucharist is only "a law," not a means of life, not an experience
of the community of faith and salvation, not a celebration
of grateful remembrance, not life from the New Covenant
and for the New Covenant!

At the Angelicum University I attended several lectures of the famous Dominican Garrigou-Lagrange, Professor of Dogmatics and Mysticism. He was also a brilliant
speaker—indeed, more brilliant still than Hürth, even if
his Latin had a French accent. However, in his entire manner he was a deliberate matador. As he came to speak of
his confrere Marin-Sola, the famous and creative dogmati-
cian and historian of dogma, whom Garrigou had banned
to the Philippines, he climbed down from the podium into
the arena in order to battle and defeat this enemy with full
corporeality. I recalled this dramatic performance very
clearly when the encyclical *Humani generis* came out, for
it affected most severely the theologians I most respected
—Marie-Dominique Chenu, Yves Congar, Henri de Lubac. Behind it there stood Garrigou-Lagrange. I could inwardly reconcile myself to him only after I heard of his
severe mental illness, which he suffered in the last years of
his life. Humanly speaking, one can never know exactly
how to distinguish between guilt and sickness.

A third experience impressed me even more deeply. I
attended several brilliant lectures on the history of law by
a layman whose name I can no longer recall. It happened

that a group of clerical students engaged this professor in a conversation before the lecture and in the process got hold of his examination grades and falsified them. They felt secure in this since this professor had notoriously poor eyesight. However, he did find out what happened. Thereupon, I heard the "lay sermon": "May God protect his Church from such dishonorable and ruthless hankerers after honors, from such self-appointed bishops-candidates who do not hesitate before crass fraud in pursuing their goals!"

I remembered this often when in examinations at the pastoral faculty of the Lateran "monsignori" came to me with my books under their arms and flattering phrases in their mouths, but with very little knowledge to show for their efforts. During one semester I issued warnings three times against such nonsense. Nevertheless, one monsignor turned up for the examination in this manner. I asked him whether he had no friend who could have warned him, and then I subjected him to an intensive examination. Grade: "unsatisfactory." I informed the Secretariat. Despite this, the man received a doctorate!

Did your Roman stay have any positive influence on your major work The Law of Christ?

Already during my first stay in Rome in 1948, I worked on my manuscript of *The Law of Christ*. My various Roman experiences strengthened my determination to struggle against a legalism which is alienated from life, to work with greater fidelity to the Holy Scriptures and to address the problems of men and women of my time.

From 1950 to 1953 I taught one semester every year in Rome at the then newly founded Academia Alfonsiana.

In the beginning, in addition to our own Redemptorist students, we had a few diocesan priests from Holland as students. I began with two courses. One dealt with "conversion" as a foundational perspective of Catholic moral theology. It was highly praised by all the students attending and its content flowed directly into my work *The Law of Christ*. The second course, the one with which I really began, had as its theme: "What can we Catholic moral theologians learn from Protestant and Orthodox Christians?" While this course was generally well received, nevertheless it was shocking to several of my listeners. They simply were not accustomed to speaking of the other parts of Christendom except in an apologetic-defensive manner. Some of them even thought: "Perhaps Father Häring is a crypto-Lutheran." I sent these students to lectures by Father Lyonnet at the Biblical Institute, who then was lecturing on what is new in the New Law, a question much discussed by the Lutheran theologians with whom I dealt. Thus my students saw that we indeed can have a great deal in common with Lutheran theologians. Nevertheless, it was only several years later that I repeated this course, and then, newly designed. I saw that one must test to see whether the time is ripe.

I worked at least ten hours every day on the manuscript of *The Law of Christ*. In Rome I had access to the non-German publications on important topics. I was grateful especially to the librarian of the Gregorian University. In Gars, Father Viktor Schurr was helpful. I needed to mention only in passing what theme I was now working on, and a couple of hours later he would bring me the best of the pertinent publications from our library; two days later would come several well-chosen works from the Munich State Library. The two professors of exegesis in Gars, Father Brandhüber and Father Schaumberger, advised me with great generosity concerning the use of the Holy Scriptures. It is hardly possible to say briefly how much help and encouragement I received from my confreres and colleagues.

In 1953 there was a sudden interruption of our painstaking struggle to establish the identity of the Academia Alfonsiana. The founder Father Buijs died suddenly. The subsequent General Chapter stood firmly behind the plan of the deceased visionary, but noted correctly that we had need of a larger number of the best prepared professors. Thus there followed a four year pause for fundamental preparation, which in the end proved fruitful.

This pause was also valuable for me. It protected me from a premature departure from my home base in Germany. Through pastoral-sociological studies and publications I grew stronger in the many-leveled life of the Church in Germany, and beyond that in the German-speaking world. I also had more time to work fundamentally on the improvement and new edition of my major work, *The Law of Christ.*

How did you and others respond when the encyclical "Humani generis" was published in 1950?

It did not come as a lightning bolt out of the blue. One could already feel the pressure of the storm brewing against the so-called "New Theology." One knew of the spying on and the denunciations of "suspicious" professors. Father Garrigou-Lagrange based a portion of his accusations on the lecture notes of less than gifted students. Frankly speaking, I was very depressed. It was good for me to be away from Rome for a while. In addition to *Humani generis*, there also came repeated warnings against situation ethics. Many thought it was directed toward me in particular. Of course there is a kind of unbounded situation ethics, as for example, by the American Joseph Fletcher. But in the Vatican statements there remained no room for appreciating the cultural context and the sober solution of conflict cases in which values and norms cannot be integrated without a fine sense of the situation. This presumes a certain flexibility of norms.

In these matters did you have formal difficulties with the Holy Office?

During these years I was never officially admonished and no doctrinal trial was initiated against me at that time. Nevertheless, the Consultors of the Holy Office spoke openly about placing my moral theology work, *The Law of Christ*, on the *Index*. This rumor also reached the ears of my various publishers and aroused concern. Later, when I met with Father Franz Xaver Hürth in the Preparatory Commission of the Council, he spoke quite openly about the careful investigation of my works (above all *The Law of Christ*) by the Holy Office, adding of course that in the end no heresy was found. The hostile attitude toward my then quite cautious renewal efforts was instigated from the outside by various groups which deliberately and without interruption pressured both the Superior General of my order and the Holy Office against me. Shortly after the beginning of his pontificate, Pope John XXIII helped me in this tension by a letter to the Superior General of my order in which he praised my moral theology and still more through his many laudatory remarks in public audiences.

Had you had personal contacts with Pope Pius XII?

Over the years of his pontificate I had only one private audience with Pius XII, and it was nothing more than an expression of politeness. To be sure, I had a number of contacts. Soon after the beginning of my Roman teaching activities I learned through a highly placed member of the Congregation of Rites that a decree was expected in which all women religious with solemn vows would be required to recite the entire Breviary in Latin. My informant also provided the name of the prelate who was responsible for the matter. I set out to see him with a carefully composed Latin memorandum and a speech well prepared in Italian. I asked this zealot of a unified liturgical language, that is, Latin, whether it would be an appropriately deserved penance for him if Holy Mother the Church were to command him to pray daily three hours in Chinese. Since he hesitated to give an answer, I gave it for him.

Then I posed a second question: "Would you, with all due respect for the lofty Chinese cultural language, be convinced that this was the most appropriate school for 'praying in the spirit'?" He indignantly rejected such an idea. He promised me in the end that he would do what he could to see that the anticipated decree was not published. Thereupon I related to him something of my experiences in the refugee missions: how I literally got stomach pains when I would say Mass in beautiful Latin for these poor and forsaken people while some young girl read the readings in stuttering German.

From that time on, a contact with the Congregation of Rites developed. Father Augustin Bea (later Cardinal) offered to personally deliver to the pope a memorandum prepared by me on the use of the vernacular, at least in the Liturgy of the Word in certain circumstances, for example, in our refugee missions. At first Pius XII was very impressed. Nevertheless, a great resistance was thrown up in the Curia and the iron law of Latin remained. I was very depressed over this. The spiritual advisor at the Collegium Germanicum, who knew of our initiative and ultimate failure, consoled me with the firm assurance that I would yet experience the Eucharist celebrated in the vernacular. He spoke as a true prophet.

In the period before the Council did you have any contact with important persons in Italian politics?

While I was in Germany in the years 1953 to 1957 I had many contacts with leading persons in the German workers' unions and often would be invited to hold lectures and courses and lead discussions. But it was only after 1957, after the Italian publication of my book, *The Power and Powerlessness of Religion*, that I developed wide-ranging relations in the world of unions and politics in Italy.

Earlier I had contacts with the great Christian Democrat politician Alcide De Gasperi, who died in August, 1954. On many weekends I retreated for intensive work at his vacation house on Lake Albano, where on Sundays I celebrated the liturgy for the neighborhood—including the family of the Minister President. He never missed an opportunity to serve at the altar during Mass. I admired this extraordinary man in many respects. Despite a series of humiliations by the Vatican, he never let either his political responsibility and worldview or his joy in the faith and love for the Church go astray. He and his family remain in my most positive memories.

Precisely because at that time in my studies and in my lecture courses I was very taken up with questions of religious sociology, I wondered why the men of the Church, especially of the Holy Office, did not notice that all their authoritarian attempts to influence Italian politics had the opposite effect. I am thinking here especially of the declaration that communists should be excommunicated. It strengthened the Communist Party, and, unfortunately, the anti-clerical feelings of many. Wherever the pastor proclaimed from the pulpit instructions and stern warnings before elections the percentage for the communist and other "undesirable" parties grew.

It also greatly disturbed me that the Christian Democrats simply called themselves, or allowed themselves to be called, "the Catholics." As archbishop of Milan, Montini was very sensitive to this phenomenon. He also expressed this sensitivity in his beautiful pastoral letter, "To Those Estranged from the Church," in which he clearly said that the Church needed to ask for their forgiveness.

4

POPE JOHN XXIII AND
THE COUNCIL

With the death of Pope Pius XII, who in many respects was a great pope, Roman theology found itself in a deep crisis. Dogmatics stood entirely in the shadow of the encyclical *Humani generis*, and moral theology was sternly admonished concerning every kind of situation ethics so that enculturation as well as any real historically situated moral theology was suspect. With the promulgation of the dogma of the Bodily Assumption of Mary (1950) Marian devotion had attained the high point characteristic of Roman Catholicism across the centuries. Added to that was the widespread knowledge that Pius XII had personally experienced the miracle of the sun of Fatima.

However, there were also significant points of rejuvenation and light. The liturgical reform of Holy Week had strengthened efforts for a thorough-going liturgical renewal, despite the many prohibitions which emanated from the Vatican. The encyclical *Divino afflante Spiritu* opened the era of the biblical renewal in theology from its center out. Scholarly attention focused on the speeches of Pius XII concerning the significance of public opinion for the life of the Church and the application of the principle of solidarity in Catholic social teaching, and even in the structures of the Church. This was true at the same time that the Holy Office saw to it that dissent had to be held within quite narrow confines. Centralization, which is customary under aging popes, was strengthened by the Roman Curia. The experiment of worker priests had been broken off. For many Catholics the aristocratic, subtly educated, diplomatically schooled Pius XII was the unsurpassable model of a pope.

After the election of John XXIII I travelled to Bologna for a meeting of sociologists of religion at the house of Cardinal Lercaro with the clear awareness that our attempt to apply the principles of pastoral religious sociology was highly suspect by the Curia. I was in a train compartment with pious Roman women and heard their lamenting the transition from "Papa angelico (the angelic pope) to this fleshly Pope John," a transition which was difficult to make. By contrast, Cardinal Lercaro and the group of pastoral and moral theologians who were interested in religious sociology saw in Pope John XXIII a great gift of God and a sign of hope.

What were the first effects of this papal election on theological research?

The announcement of an ecumenical council came like a trumpet blast. The optimism of Pope John XXIII was contagious in the best sense. For those who knew the Roman situation, however, the list of bishops and theologians named to the preparatory work was at least partly a cold shower. Nevertheless, the fact that for the Preparatory Commission responsible for questions of faith and morals names like Congar, de Lubac and Häring turned up was for the optimists a promising sign, a kind of stamp of personal identity for this undertaking of the pope, especially after one learned that the pope placed these names on the list against the will of the Holy Office.

What kind of climate prevailed in this Preparatory Commission?

It was like a constant struggle between cold air and warm air fronts. As a "Roman professor" I had the advantage over many bishops and theologians coming from the outside in that it was easy for me to speak in fluent Latin and at the same time to understand the so-called "Roman style."

The first drafts which the trusted men of the Holy Office had worked out unleashed a heavy storm. I would mention as a prime example the Dogmatic Schema on Original Sin, in which the first Adam took up most of the space, while Christ was hardly given any place at all. Responding to the question of a bishop about how that was to be explained, the "editor" stated that it was obvious since "the first Adam was more decisive than the second." We were speechless.

No less shocking was the "Dogmatic Schema on Children Who Die Unbaptized." Professor Michael Schmaus, who likewise belonged to the Preparatory Commission as a Consultor, felt personally attacked and condemned. It was the firm purpose of the authoritative figures of the Holy Office to proclaim to the world through the Council that all children who died without baptism, whether born or unborn, were excluded from eternal salvation, even if they did not have to undergo any painful suffering. An exception would be made only for the Jewish children who were circumcised and then died before the time of the Church. I asked mischievously: "What then happened to the uncircumcised girls of Israel who died?" I was instructed that this is an "inappropriate question."

I looked for allies and struggled like a lion against this ideology which obviously was intended to serve the reestablishment of the early baptism of children. My effort was personally motivated. When my eldest sister had a premature birth of twins, the first, who was born alive, was baptized, while the second came dead into the world. The local pastor then instructed my sister that only the baptized child could be buried in a consecrated cemetery; the unbaptized child had no part in salvation. As a fourteen-year-old youth I swore to myself to look thoroughly into this matter later.

I protested in the Commission against the false picture of God given, which made God's universal will of salvation incredible if God allegedly levied unfulfillable conditions. At a certain point Cardinal Ottaviani declared through his Commission Secretary Father Sebastian Tromp that I could no longer speak on this question, which indeed had long since been definitively decided on by the Holy Office. I protested on the spot and said: "The Council will decide on this matter. One cannot lay an order of silence on the Commission theologians named by the pope." As I said that I noticed that Professor Schmaus packed his things together and silently left the aula. He fled back to Munich and said to my Provincial: "I doubt whether Father Häring will survive the Council."

I survived the Preparatory Commission on this question very well. When the referred to "Dogmatic Schema" was handed on to the Central Preparatory Commission, despite the warning by Congar and myself among others, I prepared—again in fluent Latin—counter-arguments to its teaching for three cardinals who were friends of mine, including Cardinal Döpfner of Munich. Cardinal Ottaviani and Father Tromp were subjected to a careful examination on three fundamental truths: God's universal will of salvation, the saving death of Christ for all, and overabundant redemption. The Central Commission thereupon ordered that this Schema be irrevocably remanded to the archives. A primary lesson: It is worthwhile struggling.

A second experience was no less enlightening than this one, and, for the progress of the Council, one which had even greater consequences. My colleague Archbishop Maxim Hermaniuk, from the Ukrainian-Ruthenian Uniate Church, was the first to courageously bring up the topic of collegiality. The reaction of the combative troops of the Holy Office was anything but nonviolent. The archbishop, a gifted exegete, was grievously insulted.

After that thought-provoking session of the Theological Preparatory Commission, I immediately turned to Yves Congar for assistance in a defense. His response was prompt: "This concerns the great theme of this Council!" Thereupon I turned to Henri de Lubac. I saw tears in his eyes. He also felt that here the great question had been laid on the table. Since *Humani generis* he had been banned to a convent without a scientific library. Therefore he did not feel himself capable of immediately composing concrete suggestions.

Concerning the theme of the climate, there was a third experience. As Bishop Stohr took part for the last time in a session of the Preparatory Commission, he expressly encouraged me not to lose courage but to struggle on "so that the rope around the neck of the faithful will not be pulled so tight that they can draw no more air."

How did the Preparatory Commission deal with questions that affected moral theology?

Two Subcommissions of the Preparatory Commission were formed, one with the name "De ordine morali" (Concerning the Moral Order) and a second, "Chastity, Virginity, Marriage and the Family." At first I was excluded from both—certainly not by accident. The spokespersons of these two Subcommissions were the two Consultors of the Holy Office, Franz Xaver Hürth (under Pius XII, papal advisor on all moral questions and, as mentioned, with his confrere Vermeersch the main editors of the encyclical *Casti connubii*) and Hermenegild Lio (who not long ago published a thousand-page book with the Vatican Press in which he argued that the strict interpretation of the teachings of *Casti connubii* and *Humani vitae* are the infallible dogma of the Church).

By the time I was eventually called to participate in both of the subcommissions (because of action from above), the drafts were already finished. The Schema on the Moral Order followed the decision that the word "love," since it was ambivalent, was to be replaced by the concept "duty." That the Schema also contained a condemnation of Teilhard de Chardin did not surprise me, but it called forth my vigorous counter-response, which in the total Commission found an effective echo in de Lubac. But I was even more astonished that Augustine, who in the Schema on Marriage, as in *Casti connubii*, had been called upon as the crown witness for the tradition, was nevertheless post-factum to be condemned because of his saying "Ama, et quod vis fac."

First of all I referred to St. Alphonsus who in most of

his larger spiritual writings employed this word "love" with emphasis and in his beautiful book *Learn to Love Jesus* showed that the true way to know Jesus is to know true love. Hence, there should be no turning away from Jesus toward the teaching of duty by Kant. Then I suggested a wager that the citation as given would not be found in Augustine—Augustine in fact wrote: " Dilige, et quod vis, fac." "Learn to distinguish true love, and then do what true love wishes."

Matters were even worse in the draft on "Chastity, Virginity, Marriage and the Family." Concerning marriage there was the extraordinary sentence: "It is forbidden to say that love is essential for marriage." Probably in the back of the mind of the editor there was the canonical difficulty experienced in marriage cases where the presence or absence of love was difficult to prove. Nevertheless, in its general formulation this statement was an unheard of scandal for Christians.

I put forth a counter-proposal which proceeded from the basis of true love and I received from Father Tromp an hour's time to develop it. The reaction of Father Hürth was very sharp in tone: "All that stands in contradiction to the doctrine of the Church!" I then responded, "Then I can of course leave." Father Tromp assured me that my suggestion would be seriously discussed. At the end of the stormy session I helped Father Hürth, who was already quite frail, put on his coat and supported him going down the worn out steps of the palace of the Holy Office. He was obviously very touched by this gesture. Before we went out through the wrought iron gate he stopped and stood and said (in content if not verbatim) "I hope that you can understand my vigorous reaction; for I had to argue a whole day long with Pius XI who wanted to bring the very same idea into his encyclical *Casti connubii*." Certainly I could sympathize with him in this, but my ears perked up far more concerning certain Church documents.

As John XXIII made his first visit to the palace of the Holy Office, Cardinal Ottaviani presented Father Hürth as "the pillar of the Holy Office." The pope asked who this pillar might be and how his name was spelled, and then walked on. Father Hürth, according to the statement of colleagues, went home very depressed.

To what degree and in what way did John XXIII have an influence on the preparatory work of the Council?

On this a whole book would have to be written. I think a small episode can give a good indication. In an audience for all those who took part in the preparatory work of the commissions John XXIII read aloud in a very boring manner a rather dry text. Then suddenly he set it aside and said, "Now I have a very personal word to say: Never forget, the Church is not a museum!"

On the eve of the Council what were the prospects for renewal?

Of the altogether seventy drafts, I gave only the Schema on Liturgical Renewal a realistic chance. After the close of the preparatory work I was asked by Cardinals Suenens and Döpfner to seek out contacts with bishops who were friendly to me, above all Latin Americans and North Americans, in order to test the waters. Immediately before the Council we met again. I spoke of my firm conviction that except for the one on the liturgy none of the seventy texts had a chance of gaining two-thirds of the votes. Cardinal Suenens thereupon described me as a "hopeless optimist." Later he granted that I was right.

When soon thereafter Archbishop Lèon Duval of Algiers asked me to give an evaluation of the two drafts on questions of moral theology to the French-speaking bishops of Africa I was no longer so completely optimistic. I had said that I would gladly take up his invitation if he would promise me that after the Council I could preach the Gospel somewhere in Africa; for I told myself that after the Council I would no longer be able to teach in Rome if a large portion of these seventy drafts were accepted more or less as is. I related that a devout man working on the Commission had warned me about my efforts to make small improvements, for I could thereby make myself jointly guilty if these fundamentally useless drafts were ultimately accepted by the Council.

I began my first lecture before the African bishops with the citation from Paul Claudel: "Certainly we love Jesus; but nothing in the world will bring us to love moralism." Several members of the Holy Office, who are still alive, chided me because of my lectures before the bishops. They believed that everyone who was allowed to participate in the preparatory work was thereby obliged to work for the acceptance of the texts.

How did things go in the election of the members of the Council Commissions?

The Curia had lists of suggestions circulated which practically corresponded to the Preparatory Commissions'. Attentive bishops noticed the purpose and were "put out of joint." Cardinal Liènart from Lille and Cardinal Frings from Cologne took the position of spokespersons. On the day on which the election was to take place they spoke openly for a postponement so that the Council Fathers would have time to consult among themselves.

They received a spontaneous applause. My friend Loris Capovilla, at that time the private secretary of John XXIII, reported to me shortly thereafter how excited and happy the pope was over this turn of affairs. When I learned that the Italian bishops were split into three groups and could arrive at no common list, I asked Cardinal Frings if he would place several excluded Italian bishops on the lists of the North and Middle Europeans and the Latin Americans. That in fact happened, and all were thus elected. I was very much afraid that there would be a great displeasure in the Italian episcopate if hardly any Italians were chosen for the Council Commissions.

How did the first session for the Conciliar Commission for Faith and Morals go?

Absolutely stormy! Every one of the top men of the Holy Office (Ottaviani, Parente, Tromp) spoke for nearly half an hour on the moral obligation of the members to accept the prepared text, with perhaps small improvements, and to push it through the Council. The atmosphere was charged. Then Cardinal Lèger of Montreal stood up and said loudly: "If that is the case, then I see no reason for remaining here," and began to go to the door. All three ran after him and pleaded with him to remain. They insisted that he had misunderstood. They did not wish to limit the freedom of anyone. With that the ice was broken.

During the Council did you have contact with Polish bishops?

All of the Polish bishops knew that a Polish parish had "stolen" me from the Russian prisoner of war camp and adopted me as their pastor. Cardinal Wyszynski was very well disposed toward me. He himself had effectively enabled the Polish publication of my work *The Law of Christ* and also made possible the translation of others of my books. I was invited at every Council session to give a lecture with discussion before the entire Polish episcopacy, followed by a dinner together. The Cardinal said on one such occasion that the Polish bishops would gladly send Polish students to the Academia Alfonsiana since they would return from there strengthened in faith and the life of prayer.

What contacts did you have with Pope John XXIII?

I never asked for an audience. Nevertheless, he let me know through his secretary Msgr. Capovilla how very much he appreciated my efforts for the renewal of moral theology. Soon after his address at the opening of the Council I presented before the French-speaking bishops a commentary and attempted to draw from his remarks the lines of direction for the Council. From this commentary there soon appeared my book *Il Concilio nel segno dell'unità* (Rome: Ed. Paolini, 1963; *The Johannine Council, Witness to Unity*, Dublin: Gill and Son, 1963) and through a friend I had it delivered to the pope. On the day on which John XXIII signed the encyclical *Pacem in terris* he wrote in his diary: "With agreement and great pleasure I have read Father Häring's *Il Concilio nel segno dell'unità*." At that time he also let me know his feelings. Msgr. Capovilla obtained through me a number of copies, which the pope gave to his visitors. There is no doubt that the pope was firmly convinced of the necessity of a fundamental renewal of moral theology. He knew my moral theological work, *The Law of Christ*, and valued it.

I was especially happy when John XXIII handed over the revision of the text on Holy Scripture and Tradition to a mixed commission in which the Secretariat for Christian Unity was heavily represented. With this he underlined his commitment to a thinking that was ecumenical through and through.

At this time did you have any contact with Cardinal Montini?

For myself, I never sought such contacts. They happened by chance in the time before the Council when twice a month I held spiritual conferences at the Collegio Lombardo, where Cardinal Montini lived during his frequent visits to Rome. Whenever he could, he took part in my conferences, and usually afterwards we had an evening meal together. There conversation about the Council happened of itself. Montini was a most careful listener. Our conversation was especially intensive when a book by Father Lombardi appeared with very concrete suggestions and soon was criticized by the *Osservatore Romano*. I said to Cardinal Montini quite openly that I agreed with my friend Father Lombardi on all points and asked him to support the positions represented by Lombardi. I did this myself with great emphasis, particularly in my next lectures at the Pastoral Institute of the Lateran before several hundred priests. News of this soon circulated in Rome. I do not doubt that Montini did what he could in the same direction in his own diplomatic style.

5

THE COUNCIL AND POPE PAUL VI

What was the mood like during the first Council session period?

The public sessions of the first period of the Council and the work in the commissions accurately reflected the fundamental desires and the tone set by Pope John XXIII at the opening. After the ice had been broken by the frankness of Cardinal Lèger in the Theological Commission, a loosened atmosphere quickly developed. The secretary of the Council Commission and the right hand of Cardinal Ottaviani, Father Sebastian Tromp, still followed his custom of wanting to break off or hinder an undesirable discussion with the statement: "Concerning that there is no need for any discussion, for it is most certain (*certissimum*)." The bishops looked at me and I asked Tromp: "Granted that it is most certain, I would nevertheless like to ask whether it is in fact certain." As a result of the generally humorous atmosphere, at long last this repeated statement disappeared. In time the "grace of doubting" triumphed. Also, Pope John had at last succeeded in making Karl Rahner a *peritus* (expert) on the Theological Commission. Cardinal Ottaviani's attempt to treat him more or less as a silent guest collapsed and the Cardinal finally put a good face on it all.

The main work of the Commission during the first session and in the following period was to carry through a radical restructuring of the text on the Church. It began now no longer with the Pope and Curia, but with a total vision of the People of God, the Pilgrim Church, the Community of Faith and Salvation. This rethinking was difficult for some to get through their heads. Cardinal Ottaviani argued time and again that the Commission should begin the text with the Church, that is, with the Pope and Curia, and only then speak of the faithful. Each time a response was given by Bishop Schröffer (later a Curia Cardinal): "Your Eminence, even the pope and the cardinals are numbered among the faithful." Subsequently it demanded a constant critical attentiveness in order to avoid in all the conciliar texts an identification of the Pope and Curia with "the Church." It appears to me that even today there are still some people who come to grief with "the Church," even leave the Church, because by Church they still understand mainly the Curia and Vatican.

The fourth chapter in the *Constitution on the Church*, on the active role of the laity in the Church, had also developed its decisive perspectives and statements before the death of John XXIII. The Finalizing Commission worked during the summer heat in Santa Marta on the text of the fifth chapter, which dealt with the general vocation to holiness—as Pope John faced his final death struggle.

After the death of the beloved and honored initiator of the Second Vatican Council, I had no doubt that the Council would be continued in a like spirit. As a successor, only Montini and Lercaro were possibilities. Lercaro "rescued" himself by constantly calling attention to the precarious condition of his health. Montini, as his predecessor certainly had expected, became the successor, thus insuring a powerful continuation of the Council in the same spirit.

In your opinion what were the most difficult points in the subsequent Council sessions?

In my eyes the decisive issues were the ecumenical viewpoint and as a consequence the question of collegiality; then also the role of the laity, the relationship between the Church and world, and not last—and precisely in that context—the question of religious freedom.

It was the contribution of Pope Paul VI, the three Moderators (Döpfner, Lercaro and Suenens), and the Central Commission that the original seventy texts were reduced to thirteen and the themes were well chosen. The Council now had a clear goal before it. A clear "yes" was given to the fundamental reform of the Church within the view of the prayer of Christ that "all may be one," a "yes" to viewing the Church within the context of the history of salvation, a "yes"—if not always thought through to the end—to the fundamental statement of John XXIII that the doctrine of the Church is a thoroughly pastoral theology, a theology of salvation. In the Council Commission for Faith and Morals a clear majority expressed itself in this direction. Nevertheless there remained to the end a numerically small but persistent group to whom a rethinking seemed absolutely impossible. Their view was that God wanted a church which praised long-suffering.

The leading members of the Holy Office were too firmly fixed in a thought model which inclined them to centralization and absolute control. They remained largely within the mentality of those who have to defend a fortress which possesses all truth.

And the questions: collegiality, the synodal constitution of the Church?

The efforts for a collegial understanding of the Church were profoundly conditioned by a deepening of pneumatology, through a great trust in the Holy Spirit who worked in all and through all and offered gifts of grace (charisms) everywhere abundantly. In trust in the Spirit and with the power of an unrestricted "yes" to the "law of grace" one can and must dare to draw away from an all too institutionalized, centralized ensuring of "unity." Time and again admonitions and encouragements in this sense came from the observers of the Orthodox Churches. Cardinal Garonne at the Extraordinary Synod of Bishops twenty years after the Council rightly spoke of a deep, joyful conversion experience, which, at the same time, also required patient struggle.

Throughout, Paul VI represented the line of patience. He could, for example, wait for a decisive vote on the questions of collegiality and religious freedom, even when a two-thirds majority had long been assured. He wished no division into victors and defeated. And the great majority of the Council Fathers followed him in this nonviolent thinking.

The struggle for the right understanding and extent of the collegiality between the pope and bishops, and analogously between the bishop and the presbyterium, and the pastor and the congregation, was difficult; for the thought-models which had so deeply and for so long embedded themselves could not be changed overnight.

Typical in this regard was the frequent saying that the collegiality of the bishops could be manifested only "under the pope and never without the pope." In the end, a half-dozen such passages were eliminated, but there still remain more than enough. In order to mediate, Pope Paul VI, in the well-known "nota praevia," delivered an explanatory prior remark which once again lifted up the primacy of the pope in the strongest terms. Those who strongly emphasize centralism and the power of papal primacy refer to these texts without a consideration of the dynamic of the conciliar statements and their ecumenical goal.

How did you experience the bitter struggle around the presentation of the document on religious freedom?

The typically Roman theology maintained that the state fundamentally everywhere had to acknowledge the Catholic religion as the state religion, for only the truth, the full truth of the Catholic Church, had right on its side. One could on the other hand, where the Catholic Church had to struggle for its toleration and its recognition as a free minority, put forth the hypothesis of religious freedom, but indeed only as a pragmatic hypothesis. This position had brought the Church discredit in the modern world. This was felt above all in the United States, and it was from there that the most decisive fighters for religious freedom—as a fundamental thesis, and not as a second level hypothesis—came.

One of the most decisive fighters with a sharp theological understanding was the Jesuit John Courtney Murray. For almost twenty years he had been forced into silence by the Holy Office, but he appeared as an influential *peritus* at the Council and was in the Secretariat for Christian Unity as the main editor for the conciliar text on religious freedom. However, before the public discussion in the conciliar aula, the text had to be reviewed and evaluated by the Doctrinal Commission of the Council. For this purpose a subcommission was chosen. The task of coordinating secretary fell to me. The subcommission did not water down the text, but rather strengthened it.

In view of this situation Cardinal Ottaviani, the President of the Doctrinal Commission, tried delaying tactics. Since the admonitions from our side accomplished nothing, we had to request a decisive action by Pope Paul VI that forced Cardinal Ottaviani to place the text on the table for discussion in the full Commission as soon as possible. For this the bishops brought Father Murray along. Nevertheless Ottaviani refused to let him speak, despite loud protests from bishops. Since I had been chosen as speaker for this draft, I could not be refused the opportunity to speak. To my pressing request that Murray finally should be allowed to speak, Ottaviani responded angrily that one did not need this whole text since there was already too much freedom in the Church. Now my patience was tested to the limits. I said: The fact that the head of the Holy Office answers thus is sufficient proof of the pressing need of this declaration and the necessity to allow the theologian whom he had so long condemned to silence the opportunity finally to speak. Ottaviani grimly relented. It was a pleasure to experience how magnificently Murray presented his viewpoint in beautifully fluent Latin and with sovereign dignity. The subsequent vote resulted in the overwhelming majority approving the strengthened text and passing it on to the Council.

As our work was completed and we went to the elevator to go down from the top floor of the Vatican, it happened that Cardinal Ottaviani and I were standing facing each other. I said to the Cardinal: "That was an interesting day for us. We now find ourselves in the same elevator and live in the same tower. Each of us has a view from a window and sees only a part of reality." "Yes, so it is," responded my neighbor, "and in addition each of us has on a pair of glasses with colored lenses." At once Ottaviani was completely relaxed and we subsequently had a long and good conversation.

Pope Paul subjected our American friends and several others to a difficult test of patience as he repeatedly postponed the vote on the *Declaration on Religious Liberty*. In reality he thereby remained true to his programmatic encyclical *Ecclesiam suam* about dialogue as the way to find the truth. The possibility for dialogue had to be completely exhausted precisely at this turning point. Despite his efforts, Archbishop Lefevbre and his followers foundered exactly on this conciliar document. Indeed many curial members in the Vatican could come to accept it only in limited fashion.

The counter-argument persistently put forth the following thesis: "Error has no right. It can be tolerated only where a Catholic minority is dependent on the tolerance of the majority." In order to explain the distinction between the two mentalities which encountered each other here, an extensive questionnaire on the sociology and psychology of a monopoly society on the one side and an existential phenomenology of the search for truth and a non-violent witnessing to a recognized truth on the other would be needed. I attempted to undertake this particularly in the second volume of my work *Free and Faithful in Christ*, which bears the subtitle "The Way of Humanity to Truth and Love."

Those who for decades professionally and almost exclusively controlled the correct belief of fellow Christians without responsibility to any earthly agency, who excluded as well all doubt even in the area of the non-revealed truths, such persons will never be able to approach this important document of the Second Vatican

Council. This is likewise true for the *Decree on Non-Christian Religions.*

What other conciliar texts were you able to influence in their formulation?

Every Council Father and every peritus could either himself or with the help of another take a position on every text. I actively collaborated by way of constructive criticism and concrete suggestions for improvement on all the documents which went through the Doctrinal Commission. The more precise these were and the more obviously they fit into the flow of the thought and dynamics of the documents, the greater was the chance of accomplishing something. Various bishops took advantage of my services as a Latinist. In doing this the exact meaning and direction of the various suggestions were discuused. During the four Council sessions as well as the in-between periods I was often invited by entire episcopacies to hold lectures and discussions concerning one or more conciliar texts.

I was personally very interested in chapter four of the *Constitution on the Church, Lumen gentium,* on the role of the laity. The main responsibility for this significant text belonged to Professor G. Philips from Louvain. During the second-last voting when many far-reaching suggestions for improvements and changes were made, the Commission made me responsible for a careful revision which would take the most important requests into account. I first of all took up the suggestion of several Council Fathers to reformulate the text in a more Christocentric manner. Thus, the participation of the faithful was dependent not only on the salvific mission of the Church but even more precisely on the prophetic high-priestly office of Christ and his royal freedom which fulfilled itself in obedience. The improved text was almost unanimously approved.

When in the next-to-last vote on priestly formation (*Optatam totius*), many Council Fathers demanded a clear prohibition of legalistic books on moral theology, the responsible Commission asked me to try to deal with these requests. At first I presented my doubts about condemnations: for then one would have to carefully describe what one was condemning, and not much would be gained thereby. Thus I formulated the following constructive suggestion: "Special care should be given to the perfecting of moral theology. Its scientific presentation should draw more fully on the teaching of Holy Scripture and should throw light upon the exalted vocation of the faithful in Christ and their mission to bear fruit in love for the life of the world" (No. 16). The text was presented for its own vote and was almost unanimously approved.

How and to what extent did you collaborate in the formulating of the Constitution on the Church in the Modern World (Gaudium et spes)?

When toward the end of the first Council session we had to come to a clarification concerning the goal and the limits of suggestions, Cardinal Suenens and Cardinal Montini made similar motions. The Council may not remain within the circle of the inner life and institutions of the Church. It had to concern itself much more with its mission and relationship to the world of today. A subcommission in Rome attempted to work out a draft from the material of the pre-conciliar texts, but it really satisfied no one. Thus Cardinal Suenens called together a group of outstanding theologians in Malines, including Karl Rahner. Their draft was doubtless better than the first. During the second Council session in a joint meeting of the Doctrinal Commission and the complete Commission for the Lay Apostolate, that is, in a Joint Commission—which from then on was supposed to be responsible for the project "The Church in the Modern World"—there was a vigorous discussion about which of the two texts should be used as the starting point for further work. After an initially boring discussion things warmed up—and so did I.

I said more or less the following: "Why this gigantic outpouring of energy on theories and speculations? What is at stake here is nothing less than our helping to shape history and the world, and hence we should above all focus on understanding this world and 'the signs of the times.' " Completely exhausted and rather discouraged, I returned home after the coffee break. I had hardly arrived when I received a call from the Commission that I had been chosen by a large majority to serve as the coordinating secretary for the editorial committee. "You are being asked to accept the election." I was speechless. I had no illusions about such a thorny task, but nevertheless, after brief reflection, I said, yes.

Already at the first meeting of the editorial committee we were clear about the first programmatic sentence, which remained unchanged: "The joy and hope, sadness and fear of the men and women of today, especially the poor and oppressed of all types, are also the joy and hope, sadness and fear of the disciples of Christ."

At the working meeting which took place in Zurich in February, 1964, a first draft found general approval. My suggestion to proceed from the signs of the times, the signs of the presence of God in the world, but then also to take the alarming signs absolutely seriously, was also approved by Bishop Guano (from Livorno), an open and learned man, as well as by other members of the editorial committee. They agreed with the further suggestion to lay out a more fundamental prescription for the relationship of Church and the world in view of the mission of the Church for the world, in four important thematic units, namely, marriage-family, culture, politics and peace-justice. I was given the difficult task of writing a concrete draft along these lines, always with a view to the signs of the times.

The Zurich text was thoroughly discussed in a constructive manner at the plenary session of the mixed commission of sixty bishops and a like number of theologians and laity, and in certain places it was favorably improved. There was not enough time for a thorough discussion of the details of the four concrete fields of responsibility; consequently these were passed on to the Council Fathers as an "Annexus" (appendix) for study.

The basic text was approved in a general vote by the Council Fathers as a basis for further work. In this process of course valuable criticisms and concrete suggestions for improvements surfaced.

The appendix on marriage and the family pleased many Council Fathers. Still, it was vigorously attacked by Cardinal Heenan of England. His temperamental criticism was directed against my work by name. At the time Cardinal Cento, who was very friendly toward me and was the President of the Commission for the Lay Apostolate and Co-president of the project "The Church in the Modern World," called to my attention that there were evil machinations against me, and likewise that false charges against me were being laid before the Pope. I did not take that seriously.

An intervention from the side of Cardinal Bea was significant. He correctly admonished that the Commission, despite its large number of sixty bishops, was not representative enough when one looked at the world today. Almost all of the members came from the "first world," while the "second and third worlds" were only weakly represented. Bishop Guano and I appreciated this criticism and we presented a list of bishops from the "third world," like Helder Camara from Brazil, Zoa from Cameroon, Auxiliary Bishop Wojtyla from Poland. Pope Paul gladly approved adding these bishops to the Commission. Their collaboration was in general very much appreciated.

On the basis of the text from Zurich and the thoroughgoing emphasis on the signs of the times, ahistorical theologizing appeared to be overcome. Nevertheless, in the Joint Commission loud voices were raised against the concept of the signs of the times and the high value placed on it. A specific subcommission was set up to discuss the question. In a new revision, to which open-minded capable theologians like Msgr. Hauptmann (a Frenchman), Father Tucci, Msgr. Charles Moeller, and Father Hirschmann contributed valuable work, the phrase "the signs of the times" disappeared. It returned, however, ultimately strengthened as Paul VI missed no opportunity to speak of the significance of the signs of the times. The credit for the prevailing of this viewpoint belongs most of all to Paul VI. I then concentrated my work on the chapter concerning marriage and the family and the corresponding subcommission.

For two weeks in February, 1965, an intensive session of various subcommissions took place in Ariccia. For the first time women also participated—I had invited them with the approval of Bishop Guano. It was a calculated hurry-up job on my part. However, the invitation was not withdrawn, and the women made a significant contribution.

When almost two hundred bishops had demanded a formal rejection of communism, Msgr. Glorieux, secretary of the Secretariat of the Lay Apostolate and co-secretary of the large mixed commission, and I were particularly attacked as scapegoats. I have no reason to deny that I did my utmost to avoid such an obviously political-sounding condemnation. I pointed out in the discussion that a theological wrestling with the total situation was more pressing and that if one wished to condemn communism as a political and economic-social movement and ideology, a clear analysis of its drastically varying versions would have to be provided. In the back of my mind there was the clear knowledge that Pope John had given the authorities in Moscow assurance that the Council would undertake no condemnation of communism so that the participation of observers from the Russian Orthodox Church would thereby be possible.

From then on, besides Bishop Guano, Cardinal Garonne and Msgr. Philips were the decisive figures in the completion of the *Pastoral Constitution on the Church in the Modern World*. I was happy to be able to step more into the background. The matter was in the best of hands.

In addition to the work on the Subcommission on Marriage and the Family, I was to the end heavily engaged in the text on peace. I did everything humanly possible to bring about a strong statement on the right of conscience for conscientious objectors and a recommendation of non-violent defense. The results fell short of my expectations. Nevertheless, it was a beginning. Then when the penultimate voting on the total text of *Gaudium et spes* came up, I once more saw a chance. I worked through a good fifty text-improvements, fitting them very carefully into the text. Many friendly bishops, and even cardinals, especially the bishops from our congregation, accepted these suggestions for improvement (*juxta modum*) with complete confidence. No one in the subcommission, which had to review and approve the suggestions, or the full commission, knew that they came from me. Since, however, they all fitted precisely into the text, all but two made it through—above all a significant improvement in the article on conscience.

Could you say something more detailed about the conflicts that arose during the course of the discussion on Gaudium et spes *concerning the difficult question of marriage? These conflicts could perhaps provide an insight into the later tensions that surfaced on the occasion of the encyclical* Humanae vitae, *and persist even to the present day.*

The conflict with Cardinal Heenan I already mentioned. I would like to add that, with the approval of Bishop Guano and the rest of the authorities, I was able to gain the collaboration of one of the most conservative English bishops and later still another no less conservative adherent of *Casti connubii* in the work of the subcommission. To my great surprise, they all came to open-minded positions very quickly, completely in line with the text which ultimately was approved by the great majority of the Council. Near the end Professor Schillebeeckx also provided a very valuable contribution in the subcommission. A joint session was arranged between the members of the Council Subcommission on Marriage and the Family and the experts of the Papal Special Commission on Problems of Marriage and Population. There was a majority consensus.

In the last vote in which the Council Fathers could vote with a yes or no or with a yes *juxta modum*, there were suggestions for improvements in the sense of the to-

tal text. Well over two-thirds of the votes were unconditional yes votes; the votes of yes *juxta modum* were not
very numerous. The text seemed to have arrived at a safe
port. Nevertheless, a dangerous conflict arose.

Before the last vote in the Council aula powerful
voices, including Patriarch Maximos of the Melchites, Cardinal Suenens and Cardinal Lèger among others, spoke
out with the greatest possible clarity against the severe
condemnation of all contraception in *Casti connubii*. One
could sense that the majority likewise felt similarly. Then,
however, upon orders from above, the discussion on this
theme had to be broken off. Some in the Vatican would
have gladly made me the scapegoat for these speeches.
But they had no basis to do so. In fact, only Patriarch Maximos had spoken with me, as he had on other matters. I
helped in the editing of his intervention, but he had long
since formed his opinion independent of me on the basis of
the completely different mentality of the Eastern
tradition.

Since at that point the *modi* (suggestions for improvement) of the Council Fathers on this chapter had already
been responded to—a portion of them being accepted and
a portion rejected—there came a *modus* which would
have radically overturned the entire text, like a bolt out of
the blue, sent over by the Pope himself. According to the
regulamento firmly established by the conciliar popes
John XXIII and Paul VI, this was unacceptable. In the case
of a text approved by a majority (over two-thirds) no
modus may be taken into consideration if it goes fully contrary to the established direction. I had every reason to
presume that in the final voting a text which followed the
rigoristic line of *Casti connubii* would have been voted
down by a large majority—to say nothing at all about a

hardly explainable deviation from a fundamental Council rule.

I awakened Cardinal Lèger very early in the morning and gave him for his free disposal a page of text with a clear stand and the argumentation for it. He read it walking back and forth in a very excited condition and said to me: "Yes, I will move in exactly this direction."

In fact in the stormy session of the full Commission Cardinal Lèger brought forth that text in emphatic fashion. Cardinals Brown, Parente, Ottaviani and other men of the Holy Office stiffened themselves with the saying: "The pope has spoken. *Causa finita!* Contradiction is inadmissible." As the discussion was reaching the boiling point I quietly left the hall. Archbishop Zoghby, the Patriarchal vicar of the Melchites, ran after me and warned me against cowardly flight. He let me go only after I told him that it was my purpose to seek, through the Secretary of State, an audience with the Pope to request a clarification as to whether the writing of the Pope was a command or simply a handing on of a *modus* coming from the Holy Office. While I waited in the outer room of the Secretary of State for Archbishop Dell'Acqua, with whom I was friendly, one right after the other, Cardinal Lèger and Cardinal Roy, both Canadians, turned up. When they came, I said: "Then I can return to the discussion." Cardinal Roy then handed the Pope a letter which had been composed by the laity who had worked on the Commission. Cardinal Lèger handed the Pope the sheet which I had brought to his house early that morning.

Thereupon I participated in the still hot discussion. On the very same day there came the authoritative answer that *modi* sent to the Commission by the Pope were not commands but rather only requests for consideration. In the following days a letter from Cardinal Ottaviani fell into my hands in which the head of the Holy Office complained to the Pope that the majority of the Commission had raised strong resistance, but that several significant modifications were attained. On the photocopy the handwriting of the Pope was clear to read: it briefly and clearly responded that the decision of the Council Commission should be adhered to.

In fact several corrections and insertions were made in the Council text, which a practiced eye easily can recognize as nonorganic additions; among them was a significant footnote in which it is declared: "By order of the Holy Father, certain questions requiring further and more careful investigation have been given over to a commission for the study of population, the family, and births, in order that the Holy Father may pass judgment when its task is completed. With the teaching of the magisterium standing as it is, the Council has no intention of proposing concrete solutions at this moment" (footnote 14 to number 51). In the text there was the insertion " . . . it is not allowed to the children of the Church to undertake methods of birth control which the magisterium in its explanation of the divine law has rejected." Clearly the expression "children of the Church" falls outside the language usage of the Council. Cardinal Deardon of Detroit, as chairperson, led the work of the Subcommission on the Family and Marriage. Today I still remember with admiration his calm and firmness, and also his flexibility, naturally necessary at that time.

Among the Council Fathers, insofar as they were informed about the course of events, there prevailed a critical attitude. I can still remember how Cardinal Frings asked me whether after all that one should accept the modified text. I answered him with a yes; for with the rejection of this part the entire text of *Gaudium et spes* would be placed in question, and the end of the Council would most likely be depressing. Only now do I understand the full force of the question by Cardinal Frings and others.

The daily Italian press spoke of its assumptions about a crisis. However, as I spoke on Italian television on that critical evening, the reaction of the press on the following day was thus: There obviously can be no talk of a crisis; otherwise the relaxed attitude of Father Häring would be inexplicable.

6

THE CRISIS AROUND
HUMANAE VITAE

In March of 1963, John XXIII set up a commission of eight experts on birth control and population problems. Paul VI soon expanded this Commission to sixty-one and later seventy-five members. Would you like to say something about your experiences and reflections concerning this?

I was informed about the work of this commission by the Pope himself in connection with the retreat which, at his behest, I preached for him and the higher members of the Curia (at the beginning of Lent, 1964). He also asked of me several evaluations concerning this problem, for example, the teaching of St. Alphonsus, who was widely known as a vigorous opponent of the extreme sexual pessimism of St. Augustine.

Could you say something here about this retreat? Certainly it must have had a connection with the Council?

I shuddered when the majordomo brought me a personal letter with this commission; for I already had both hands full with work on the Council. I asked the prelate to tell me precisely with what titles I should address the Pope, cardinals, and other participants in the retreat. After he did so, I asked him to write the instructions out for me since I had no memory for matters which did not please me. With my words still echoing in his ears, he reported this to the Pope. In the audience before the retreat the Pope forbade me to waste my time and that of the others with unnecessary titles. I could, if I wished, begin: "Reverend Fathers." Otherwise, nothing. Then the Pope encouraged me: "Courage! Preach without fear! Preach the Gospel powerfully, exactly as you would otherwise!" As I then wanted to ask whether I was allowed to address delicate questions of the Council, the Pope anticipated me: "Of course, this concerns not only the salvation of our souls. You must contribute to opening up everyone in the Curia to the great goals of the Council!"

I followed the encouragement to the letter. After several lectures the papal sacristan said to me: "One does not preach thus in the Vatican! If you continue so I fear that the Pope will take you by the ears." There was nothing of the sort. Time and again I directed attention to the working of the Holy Spirit, the Paraclete. I concretized it, for example, in the liturgical reform, whereby I emphasized the proclamatory character, the *paraclesis*, and protested against the idolatry of Latin. As I left the chapel after that lecture Cardinal Bacci, the great Vatican Latinist and most zealous fighter for Latin in theology and liturgy, waited for me. The Cardinal was extremely shaken by my *paraclesis* and said first of all: "Father, pray for me: I am a great sinner!"

As a remembrance of the retreat the Pope added in Italian to the customary litany of praise the verse: "Praise to the Holy Spirit, the Paraclete (comforter-encourager)!"

Could you here give the reader a resume of your description of the teaching about marriage by St. Alphonsus which the Pope requested of you?

Since in the encyclical *Casti connubii*, paralleling the Augustinian interpretation of the *finis procreatione* (goal of procreation) the moral, rigoristic norm was one-sidedly specified, I quoted the view of Alphonsus, which was diametrically opposed. The latter spoke of a threefold purpose of both marriage and also the marriage act: the first, absolute and indispensable purpose is always the mutual giving and strengthening of the indissoluble bond of loyalty. Then follow the two purposes of marriage which are internal to marriage, but nevertheless only accidental to it: procreation and the satisfaction of the sexual drive. These of course may never arbitrarily be excluded, but they cannot and need not be activated in every marriage and in every marriage act. This view influenced also the casuistry and the moderation shown to married persons in these questions.

How was the papal commission on population problems and the regulation of conception constituted?

It was doubtless an interesting group from which one could learn a great deal. There belonged to it demographers, marriage counselors, psychological therapists, and members of Christian family movements. I am thinking especially of the sympathetic and committed founders of the Christian Family Movement in the U.S.A., Mr. and Mrs. Crowley. In the end there were something over twenty theologians among the seventy-five members. The Auxiliary Bishop Reuss of Mainz should be particularly mentioned for he was already known as an advocate of turning away from the rigorism of the encyclical *Casti connubii*.

His appointment by Paul VI had a background: as Bishop Reuss distributed a petition in St. Peter's Square against the acceptance of the weak document on the means of communication, the General Secretary of the Council, Archbishop Felici, wanted to prevent him from doing so; he tore the paper out of his hands, whereby Bishop Reuss, a war invalid with a prosthesis, stumbled to the ground. Upon the request of the Pope, Bishop Reuss waived his legal right to a charge against Felici. On his side, the Pope wanted to honor him by naming him a member of the papal commission. There he was a successful dialogue partner.

At the beginning of our work the majority of the sixty-one and then seventy-five members doubtless were on the rather conservative side, that is, they did not wish to retract the norms of *Casti connubii*, but rather declared themselves in favor of pastoral modification and flexibility. Indeed for many years that was also my position—of course, no longer so at the time that I was called to the papal commission. I had decided firmly in favor of the Alphonsian line; that is, briefly stated: Every marriage act must be an expression of marital love and a promotion of marital loyalty, but in no way must every marital act be directed to procreation.

However, since in one of his several audiences the Pope encouraged the members of the commission to search honestly and in an unhindered way for solutions which were in keeping with the truth, the weight shifted of itself. In the end, only four theologians, the Jesuits Zalba, Ford, and Lestapis and the Dutch Redemptorist Jan Visser, remained fundamentally in the line of *Casti connubii*. Lestapis and Visser, however, wanted a milder pastoral approach. Ford and Zalba fixated themselves firmly on that encyclical. All four theologians granted at a certain point that from the matter itself they were not able to give any firmly convincing argumentation. Ford above all emphasized a fundamental motive: It is unthinkable that the Holy Spirit could have been more with the Anglican bishops in 1930 than with the Roman Church—unthinkable, therefore, that, after all, the Catholic Church could accept what the Anglican bishops had taught in 1930, to the irritation of Rome.

Zalba argued emotionally: "What then about the millions of souls which according to the norms of *Casti connubii* we have damned to hell, if those norms were not valid?"

The lovable Mrs. Crowley answered casually: "Do you really believe that God has carried out all your orders?"

Did the Commission then in the end wish to have the Pope approve the "pill"?

One cannot often or clearly enough state that the papal commission was not a pill-commission, and that it in no way wanted to give the Pope recommendations concerning any kind of contraceptive pills. There are many different kinds of pills, depending on their ingredients and their effect. I likewise would want to emphasize clearly that the commission did not in any way wish to recommend to the Pope any concrete method. Its aim was much more that a papal position should remain on the level of general principles without expressing any teachings on a concrete method. To be sure, the commission took as a starting point the clearly expressed declaration of Pius XII that the rhythm method was permitted in order to space births or even to avoid pregnancy altogether if it would not be a responsible pregnancy. But the majority did not want to set up a sharp opposition between naturalness and artificialness. Even in the natural method of family planning there is an element of artificialness, although of a very different sort. The recommendation of the majority of the commission remained more or less on the same level as the recommendations of the joint synod of the German dioceses in Würzburg: "The judgment concerning the method of the regulation of conception, which decision belongs to the married couple, may not be made arbitrarily, but their conscientious analysis must take into consideration the objective norms which the teaching office of the Church has put forward. The method utilized may not psychologically injure either of the two partners or restrict their capacity for loving" (Synodal Conclusions: "Christlich gelebte Ehe und Familie," 2.2.2.3). I would here especially like to call attention to the final sentence of this instruction; for here is the heart of what the majority of the Papal Commission wanted to recommend.

Again I would like to emphasize that the commission in no way wished—although this is time and again presumed—that the Pope should simply say yes to the progesterone pill. Concerning the Commission's relative hesitation concerning the so-called natural family planning method, one must also recall that at that time research on it was not nearly as developed as it is today.

How do you see the development in the two commissions (the conciliar and the papal commissions) on the one hand and public opinion on the other?

I believe that even before the Council many marriage counselors and therapists held a viewpoint that anticipated the results of the two commissions. The great majority of married people were simply "speechless" before the strict norms of *Casti connubii*. The violations were "confessed," but it could not in earnest be imagined that things would change very much. In the circles of pastoral and moral theologians one spoke of these matters only behind closed doors. Many did not dare even to think these things through critically for themselves. The control through the Holy Office and through some bishops was effective, indeed, not in bringing forth true convictions, but rather in regard to public oral expression. Only very few theologians dared in the preparatory period and during the first period of the Council to publicly raise questions and doubts. However, when men like Cardinal Suenens and Patriarch Maximos spoke out courageously in the Council, the situation changed overnight. Toward the end of the Council the news that the Pope wanted to sharpen the norms of *Casti connubii*, or that he was close to doing so under the pressure of the Holy Office, strengthened the tendency of opposing public opinion to speak up. When the report of the Papal Commission came to public light, there arose in the public a wait-and-see attitude in precisely this sense.

What happened in the slow, and then at the end rapid, turnabout in the public opinion within the Catholic Church is well illustrated by the events in England. The retired Jesuit Archbishop Roberts from Delhi, in view of the population explosion and the hunger in India, was one of the first churchmen to speak out publicly in favor of lifting the strict norms of *Casti connubii*. Since he then lived and spoke in England, the English bishops felt bound in conscience to publicly take him to task in 1964.

On this occasion a journalist of the *Manchester Guardian* called me up and asked what I thought of the matter. I told him that I would rather that the bishops had not taken a position against the retired archbishop. The journalist made this a huge headline front page: "Father Häring against the English Bishops." This was a bad way of doing things, but it does make clear the development within the public opinion on the question.

How did the final session of the Papal Commission go?
How did a minority report come about?

I must openly confess that I absented myself from the last session. There was indeed an objective reason for this. I would have had to renege on a course for Protestant pastors in the U.S.A. which I had long ago agreed to. The decisive motive, however, was the thought that I could perhaps better serve the cause through my absence. I was aware of the hostile attitude of the authoritative men of the Holy Office toward me and their tendency to make me the scapegoat for the reversal of opinion which had taken place in the Papal Commission. From the beginning the Commission was put together in such a way that a recommendation in the sense of *Casti connubii* was to be expected. I wanted to avoid violating these sensitivities. I wrote a letter to Riedmatten, the chairperson of the Commission, that everything which Father Perico, S.J., would say and how he voted, would be exactly what I would say and how I would vote. In fact, he appeared to me to be the clearest head and the most capable speaker of the progressively oriented among the theologians on the Commission.

From everything that I could find out from the participants in the Commission, there were by no means two reports in the final session; there was one and only one report, which gained a good ninety percent of the votes.

Only afterwards did the group of four theologians

named above, along with other friends of Cardinal Ottaviani, put together an opposing report. This letter was therefore neither laid before the Commission nor discussed. Also, the minority report had no signatures from the laity of the Commission. It, of course, was sent on to the Pope.

Was there not still another report which went to the Pope?

Whether one should speak of a report or not, I cannot say. The fact is, however, that as the work of the Commission came to a close, Paul VI set up a kind of control commission made up of cardinals and bishops. Among others there were in that commission Cardinals Döpfner and Heenan and Auxiliary Bishop Wojtyla, our present pope. Everyone could easily imagine the position of Cardinal Döpfner. Concerning Cardinal Heenan one assumed—presumably also the Pope—that he remained on the old strict line, for he had at the time taken part in the public position against Archbishop Roberts. Further, in the Council, in St. Peter's, he had taken a hard position against me specifically on account of this question. Nevertheless, Cardinal Heenan not only had completely reconciled himself with me, but had also more or less worked his way through to a conviction which was the same as mine.

Two-thirds of the control commission held the report of the Papal Commission to be correct; one-third were opposed. There will be hardly any doubt about the position at that time of Bishop Wojtyla. He had clearly never changed his opinion, which he expressed shortly before the Council in his book on marriage and responsibility. For him there existed only the alternative: either an orientation toward procreation (then lust can be united with love), or contraception (then it is nothing more than ani-mal lust, sinful lust).

Paul VI took a long time before giving his answer in Humanae vitae *in the summer of 1968. What happened in the meanwhile?*

So far as I could tell, Paul VI was in the beginning rather strongly impressed by the report of the Commis-sion, and especially in view of the fact that the additional "Cardinals-Bishops-Commission" held the report to be correct by a two-thirds majority. This opinion of mine seems also to be confirmed by a statement of Father Her-menegild Lio, O.F.M., for decades a Consultor of the Holy Office and a special advisor to Cardinal Ottaviani. Fran-ciscan friends of mine who lived with Father Lio in Sant' Antonio, reported to me a somewhat indiscreet statement by Father Lio. According to their report, he was able to reconvert the Pope, who was almost turned around by the report, in two audiences, organized for him by Cardinal Ottaviani.

As a side remark, it should be noted that Father Lio and Father Hürth were the chief editors of the pre-con-ciliar document on chastity, virginity, marriage and the family, in which, as already noted, it stated: "It is forbid-den to maintain that love is essential in marriage." Lio was then also, upon the order of Cardinal Ottaviani, made a *peritus* on the Council Subcommission on Marriage and the Family—until the bishops of the Subcommission de-clared that they would no longer participate as long as Lio was there.

I myself was never able to speak personally with the Pope during the entire interim period. Two or three times I attempted to get an audience and was politely told that they would let me know. However, one never took place, so I gave up my efforts. So far as I could learn, no other theologians who were co-responsible for the report in the Commission were able to either—until the Pope had spoken publicly. Perhaps the one exception was Lambruschini, who had voted with the majority in the Commission, but whom Paul VI then made responsible for the announcement of the encyclical *Humanae vitae* in a press conference. He did, as is known, state at the press conference that the Pope did not see the encyclical as an infallible and irreformable dogma.

How did you experience the publication of Humanae vitae?

I was at that time lecturing in the U.S.A. Two journalists from *Time* and *Life* sought me out about five days before the publication of the encyclical and gave me a copy of the text, with the condition that I would grant them an interview on the same day that the encyclical would be published. I asked them how they came to have the text. Answer: "It cost us only a few thousand dollars!" I took the copy of the text, but protested and rejected vigorously the condition of cooperating in a matter which obviously dealt with an immoral action. I could understand the curiosity of the journalists better than the Vatican seller of such a document. I immediately withdrew to a "house of prayer" in California and gave my address only to my superior. My aim was to pray a long time and to be silent even longer. As I read the text a good twenty times I gratefully discerned that there were also very beautiful things said about the meaning of married love. It was also clear to me that the new encyclical spoke no longer of the *crimen* (crime) of contraception. In contrast to *Casti connubii*, it contained a decriminalization. Nevertheless, the norm that every marriage act without exception must remain open to conception appeared to me as an incommunicable statement in view of the following explanation that the natural methods (probably choosing only the infertile period) were in line with this fundamental principle. I could see the crisis of conscience this would cause many people, but still I hoped that the relatively mild approach would be understood as tone-setting.

Soon after the publication of the encyclical, however, the telephone kept ringing off the hook. Somebody must have betrayed my place of retreat. Theologians, well-thought-of priests, and doctors said to me on the telephone that they were thinking about leaving the Church. Why? Many more serious injuries had occurred in Church history. Often the answer was given to me: In no less than the *Osservatore Romano* there appeared a demand by Cardinal Felici that whoever does not accept the encyclical in obedience and in belief should leave the Church. With that one blow my determination to be silent on the question was set aside. One had to fear that there would be not only an alienation from the sacraments of the Church, as happened with *Casti connubii*, but indeed a massive exodus out of the Church.

How could you as an individual, an individual fighter so to speak, hope to do something against so serious a danger?

Of course I was not at all certain that a brave attempt would be successful. Would it become a call in a many-voiced concert to remain in the Church, or would the call of an individual find only an empty echo?

I was asked whether I would sign the declaration of a

large number of American theologians who had gathered in Washington. The question was about the effectiveness of a joint action. I agreed with the heart of the declaration, namely, that there are marital situations in which following the strict norms without exception, that is, the strict prohibition of artificial birth control, may not be urged. Nevertheless, I did not want to put myself in the position of being accused of having co-organized a collective protest.

After a night spent in prayer I came to the decision that out of love for the Church I owed it to the "people of God" to express my viewpoint openly, whatever the consequences for me personally might be. I trusted in the grace of God that I could loyally and with inward calm remain within the Church, even if I would be subjected to sanctions.

Thus I issued the following declaration: "Whoever can be convinced that the absolute forbidding of artificial means of birth control as stated by *Humanae vitae* is the correct interpretation of divine law must earnestly endeavor to live according to this conviction. Whoever, however, after serious reflection and prayer is convinced that in his or her case such a prohibition could not be the will of God should in inner peace follow his/her conscience and not thereby feel her/himself to be a second-class Catholic."

On the following day my statement appeared on the front page of the *New York Times* and the most popular newspapers of other countries. I certainly had not expected that my lone voice would find such a worldwide echo. Hundreds of Catholics later assured me that because of my voice they had resisted the temptation to leave the Church.

I immediately wrote my article, "The Encyclical Cri-

sis: Contradiction Can and Must Be a Service to the Pope"
in *Commonweal* (1968, pp. 588–594). At the same time I
sent a German version to Cardinal Döpfner. The text was
immediately published in his collection of most important
statements in the Munich church newspaper. This detailed statement also found a worldwide echo. It was also
for many believers an occasion for a serious and honest
searching of their consciences and was felt by many as
liberating. Likewise my commentary on the chapter on
marriage in *Gaudium et spes* published at that time in *Das
Zweite Vatikanische Konzil, Dokumente und Kommentare
(The Second Vatican Council: Documents and Commentary*, Freiburg, 1968, vol. III, pp. 424–446) received
worldwide attention. In rapid succession there appeared
the two-volume *Brennpunkt Ehe: Heutige Probleme und
Perspektiven in Tradition und Lehramt (Love is the Answer*,
Denville, N.J., 1970) and *Krise um Humanae vitae (The
Crisis of Humanae vitae)*. Both books were quickly translated into several languages. This was probably the first
time that a pastoral and theologically critical statement
appeared in the modern communications media. In a few
weeks the bishops, theologians and "lay people" world-
wide could quickly come to an understanding of a burning
question of conscience.

Did you have contacts with bishops after your statement?

Indeed, unexpectedly many. I would like to mention
only a few. Already very early I and several other theologians were invited to an intense discussion with significant
representatives of the American bishops' conference. The
discussion took place in a truly fraternal atmosphere. I also
met with key figures of the Canadian episcopacy.

In the beginning of September I returned from North

America to Rome. I had already long since accepted invitations from the Sicilian and Sardinian bishops. After the open public statement of my opinion I wrote to the inviting bishops that I presumed that under these circumstances my coming would probably be inopportune. The answer was: "On the contrary. We wish to hear what you have to say to the pastoral situation after *Humanae vitae.*" The two-week-long course on the two islands took place in the best atmosphere and with many listeners—something that I certainly had not dared to dream.

How did your fellow Order members and your superiors react?

The Redemptorists are pastors who are close to the people. They could feel the shaking, indeed the radiating vibration like a seismograph. I can gratefully say that the great majority of my confreres and all of my superiors clearly felt that my various statements were through and through pastorally inspired. Most of them also saw that even a protest can be an expression of a great love for the Church and the Pope.

In several Order provinces, however, the transition from a partly rigoristic-casuistic moral theology to a kerygmatic-oriented one, above all among the older fathers, was not yet completed. Altogether, in three English-speaking Order provinces the English translation of my book *The Law of Christ*, despite its great success, was still enclosed in the locker of forbidden books. The result was, however, that the theology students and younger fathers had themselves given the books for presents and studied them all the more eagerly in proportion to the railings against them. A general consultor of one of these provinces, who was personally very friendly toward me, warned me very openly against visiting the houses of his province unless I was willing to let myself in for some severe criticism. When upon the urging of a friendly house superior I acted differently, I began to feel how right the general consultor was. I could completely sympathize with the older fathers. Many had with a wounded heart refused absolution to many penitents in the exact fulfillment of what *Casti connubii* said concerning confessional practice in regard to birth control. Moreover, they gradually accustomed themselves to this and were perhaps even a little proud of their radical loyalty to Church doctrine. With this attitude, many of them did not even realize that the tone of *Humanae vitae* was a completely different one from that of *Casti connubii*. In houses in which the tension and the generation gap were especially severe, not a few idealistically oriented young confreres left the congregation. Some have remained in contact with me.

Also in this critical phase, the superiors granted me a great indulgence of trust. I would only like to call attention here to the attitude of my then General Superior Amaral, who came from the Order's province of Sao Paulo, Brazil, which had been founded by the fathers in south Germany. After the public announcement of my critical position, I sent a copy of it to the Papal Secretary of State, Cardinal Cicognani. The Secretary of State called Father Amaral in and pressed him to deter me from my position and to request that I place myself unconditionally behind the statement of the encyclical. It was pointed out to him that this should be undertaken with a view to the important service which Father Häring could carry out in the Church in the future. Father Amaral answered, as he told me many weeks later: "I am only a canonist. Father Häring has a much greater competence in the field of moral theology."

    In September when I returned from North America to Rome and the Order General greeted me, he said not a word about this to me. Only two weeks later, after my trip to Sardinia and Sicily, did he speak about this and let me know that Cardinal Cicognani had invited me to a conversation. This took place as soon as possible. It was, however, not the first contact with me since my critical statements. The Vatican sought contact with me not through the Apostolic Delegate in the U.S.A., Archbishop Vagnozzi, because it was known that I was not well disposed toward him since he always had me spied upon and passed on incorrect information concerning me to the Holy Office. The Apostolic Delegate Clarizio from Ottawa was brought in for the job. He sent me a letter which was very friendly in tone in which he invited me to an early visit in Ottawa. Archbishop Clarizio personally met me at the airport and treated me like an "honored guest," heard out my argumentation that I had acted the way I did in order to prevent an exodus from the Church, and in the end personally accompanied me once again back to the airport. Cardinal Cicognani was very objectively informed through him.

    The conversation with the Cardinal Secretary of State lasted a long time and was completely candid and polite on both sides. It nevertheless was a shock to me when he told me that the Pope was especially troubled concerning my propaganda against celibacy. I rejected this as a terrible, unheard of slander and offered to provide him an entire dossier of my most recent publications and speeches about celibacy. With complete pastoral understanding for those priests who did not see themselves to be in the position to meaningfully and truly live in committed celibacy, I had always encouraged them to remain true to their freely accepted obligation. The Cardinal assured me that he believed me completely in this matter, and he would inform the Pope most carefully that here they had to deal with a sorry chapter of character defamation. Thus in the end the question concerning *Humanae vitae* slipped into the background of this important discussion. At the conclusion the Cardinal accompanied me precisely as far as was the custom with representatives of government. I was nothing less than astonished at this delicate treatment. I believe the reason for it was the deep sympathy of the Cardinal for my besmirched reputation.

Some time later the Cardinal once again took up contact with me through Archbishop Clarizio upon the occasion of his vacation trip home. He invited me to his parents' house. After a somewhat lengthy polite conversation he asked me—obviously in the name of Cardinal Cicognani—whether I now perhaps after all of the clarifications by the bishops' conferences could see myself in a position to express myself positively toward the encyclical. I then did in fact make such a frank declaration, in the sense that I acknowledged the encyclical as completely acceptable as it was interpreted by the great episcopal pastorals, and that now I could even see its positive merits better. That satisfied the Vatican completely at that time.

I also maintain precisely the same position today. My essay of January, 1989, in the weekly journal *Christ in der Gegenwart* and in *Il regno* is a reflection of this. I mean that the encyclical was received as it was explained by the declaration of the great episcopacies, and I am firmly convinced that it is neither received nor is receivable if one attempts to ram it through in light of *Casti connubii* and in an intensified struggle against those bishops' conferences.

Today, as then, I read the encyclical *Humanae vitae* in light of the Alphonsian doctrine of the application of *epikeia* in matters of inferred laws of morality—in light of the great tradition of the Orthodox Churches concerning *oikonomia*, which deepened greatly the question of *epikeia* through its pneumatology, and in light of the conclusions of the joint Synod of the West German Diocese.

Could you perhaps show in some concrete examples how you dealt with these problems in a pastoral way?

A first example lies on the level of the proclamation of morality: soon after my response to *Humanae vitae* in the summer of 1968 the pastor of one of the largest parishes in the Boston area invited me to speak to the entire parish in a gigantic community hall. It was filled to the last place. I spoke within the perspective of the Council concerning the magnanimous responsible handing on of life, concerning the astounding "fruitfulness" of married love for time and eternity, and concerning marital chastity as the nurturing of precisely this love. I spoke very briefly about a meaningful interpretation of the encyclical in precisely this perspective of the Council. I uttered a couple of sentences about the meaning of *epikeia* and *oikonomia* and the image of God standing behind them. I received a huge applause! Many said to me: "Yes, you love the Church and the Pope and also feel with us." Concerning the fruitfulness of this approach, let the baptismal register of the following years be consulted.

Also upon the occasion of the celebration of baptism, which I often undertook in America, I experienced time and again, both orally and in writing, how some married couples had renewed their desire for another child. On the occasion of a retreat for Protestant pastors and their wives, an Anglican pair came to consult with me concerning methods for family planning. I answered: "The question of the method comes only at the end! Now meditate on the word: 'What can I return to the Lord for all that he has done for me!' Think about the intimacy of your love and about the harmony of your six-person family, about the art of your raising children, about the problems of health. Only then can we sensibly speak of the question of method. And then I would also first like to hear you tell me what the two of you think and feel." Two years later they were again with me in a retreat. In the meanwhile their Sinty was born and they had adopted a handicapped black orphan child. There followed four more adoptions of difficult "mixed bloods" whom no one wanted and finally an unplanned pregnancy as the wife reached forty-two years of age.They came to me for advice because of a lesion in her uterus: should they let nature take its course since, if no intervention were undertaken at the latest toward the end of the third month, a spontaneous abortion was to be expected? We prayed together. The consulting gynecologist had said that an intervention meant no small risk and also many difficulties. Nevertheless he added: "This woman obviously has an unconquerable inner source of strength." The child which was brought into the world is today a great joy for the entire, happy family. And all that without the breath of rigorism!

We stand not under naked legalism, but rather under the rule of grace. This must be felt in all of our pastoral work.

7

THE DOCTRINAL TRIAL AND
OTHER EXPERIENCES
WITH THE HOLY OFFICE

I know from other theologians of the Council majority that you came into conflict with the Holy Office, later known as the Doctrinal Congregation. How did this happen?

You have sensed how difficult it is for me to speak publicly about things which have long been secret and which touch me in an inmost way. My hesitation certainly does not come from a desire not to burden the last years or months of my life with perhaps unnecessary difficulties. My question is above all whether it will serve the Church and the joy of faith, which we all need; whether we will do all that is humanly possible to encourage a change, a transformation of the structures and mentalities which are not gospel-centered. I believe that we have arrived at the point where it can no longer be disputed that we are in a pathological situation. This has a long history behind it.

My intensive concern with the nonviolence of Gandhi and with the therapeutic dimension of liberation theology lead me to the conclusion that at this point we are in need of *Satyagraha*, the powerful and liberating truth expressed with love. From long service as a medic I know that one must open up wounds before healing can begin.

In the spirit of Gandhi's practiced transparency, and also his *Ahimsa*, his intimate sympathy, I wish in the following discussion to lay my hands on the wounds which need a healing on the institutional level, knowing full well that all of us in the best of cases are no more than wounded healers. I trust that this will be possible for me without malice.

Is a certain triumphalism, a covering up and silencing of the humiliating conditions in the Church not a greater scandal, indeed a scandal in the moral sense, than an objective stating of the sobering truth?

You and your friends, as well as my friends, have slowly convinced me of this. In meditating on the Bible several things in this regard have become clear to me. Did not Christ himself suffer most of all because of the denials of his disciples, indeed of his apostles? Would not the specter of unhealthy and destructive Church structures which imitate worldly power and pomp have caused him pain?

Fully aware that we ourselves must always remain on the path of an ongoing conversion if we are to call for the reform of the Church, I see, however, how inauthentic the preaching of conversion on the individual level can be if one will not also participate in the constant reform of the Church and its structures. This concerns indeed nothing less than being true to the gospel, to the credibility of our witness and of the entire proclamation.

Finally and not least, the concern for the unity of Christianity also moves me. The Orthodox Churches have remained true to their faith without having an institution which would be comparable to the Roman Inquisition with a "Suprema Sacra Congregatio Sancti Officii" (What a name! "The Most High Holy Association of the Holy Office"). Did it encourage a joy in belief? Has it strengthened the happy and incarnated proclamation of salvation to all cultures and peoples? Has it encouraged an unceasing research and an always deeper thinking about the revealed truth? All these questions make me uneasy, but especially those of ecumenical interest, that the great grace of our time will not be in vain. Upon the occasion of his visit to Rome, in December, 1987, the Ecumenical Patriarch Dimitrios, with great candor, charged the Roman Curia to put the ecumenical goals at the center of all of their actions and omissions. (See *L'Osservatore Romano*, December 6, 1987, p. 4: "Looking toward the unity of Christianity should be the determining foundation for every ecclesial activity!") And time and again ecumenically involved churchmen from all parts of Christianity have admonished that most particularly certain forms of centralization and opaque exercise of authority stand in the way of reunion.

How have your often painful experiences, above all the long doctrinal trials against you, affected your work as a theologian and your personal life?

In wrestling with an answer I think first of all of the doctrinal trial concerning my writings, which ran from 1975 to 1979. It even continued for two years while I was in a life-and-death struggle against cancer of the throat. And soon after the last treatment similar difficulties with the Congregation of Studies began. Worry about it plagued me greatly for many sleepless, painful nights. I see it as a graced challenge to my faith which is able to give a meaning to all suffering. The question which moves me now during my telling of the story and my decision to make the documents available to the public is this: how can one spare others such suffering?

Looking back I believe that I can nevertheless confirm that this was the most creative period of my life. The perspective of an imminent death gave me a great inner freedom from every form of external pressure. And the pressure which the Vatican offices wanted to place me under strengthened my alertness not to commit the sin of cowardice and dissemblance in the end.

It was precisely in this period and under these circumstances that the major work of my theological effort, *Free and Faithful in Christ*, was written, which has now come out in a fourth German printing as a special edition. I myself wrote it first of all in English because the English-speaking audience is much greater than the German. It has been translated into another nine languages. This book is not a new edition of *The Law of Christ*; for since 1954, the year of the first edition of that work, the situation in the world and the Church has changed drastically and so has my thinking, influenced so much by the Council and worldwide experiences.

Without irony or sarcasm I believe that I can say that my experiences with the Holy Office, and the later Doctrinal Congregation, have had a liberating effect on me. Thus, I have in a certain sense a burden of gratitude. Would that my suggestions for reform will be seen as an attempt to express that gratitude!

Whoever loves the Church must also be prepared to suffer in the Church, with the Church, through the Church, and for the Church. Great theologians of the past and the present have given us examples of this. I think of

St. Thomas, St. Alphonsus, Antonio Rosmini, Cardinal Newman, Karl Rahner, Henri de Lubac, Yves Congar, to mention only a few.

How have you shared the suffering that other men experienced from the Holy Office?

When the doctrinal trial was thrust upon me I was somehow prepared for it by my previous sympathy with others. Indeed, their suffering was much more intense, for before the Council everyone who was struck by the lightning of the Holy Office, of Indexing or condemnation was treated as a leper in his surroundings. He was simply excluded and branded. Today, as it was at the time of my first interrogation by the Holy Office, the situation is different. Throughout the difficult years I experienced the greatest trust and constant encouragement from my Order and superiors, from many bishops and from numerous other Christians.

I remember with deep emotion how the famous exegete Professor Josef Schmidt from the Munich Catholic Theological Faculty told me how very much his joy in work had been lamed by his unfriendly experiences with the Holy Office. Fritz Tillmann, whose moral theological works had impressed me very much, was first an exegete but then voluntarily left this dangerous area to devote himself to moral theology, which at that time did not lie within the purview of the Holy Office. I was not surprised when the learned and saintly Cardinal Pellegrino characterized a typical representative of this hard line to me in this way: in such a person one could find "a complete proportionality between ignorance and arrogance." To express this differently, I would like to formulate my main concern thus: "a disproportion between bureaucratic and substantive competence."

My friend Herbert Doms came to experience this astounding disproportion as his work *Vom Sinn und Ziel der Ehe* (*On the Meaning and End of Marriage*, 1935), which was characterized by a high degree of substantive competence and balanced judgment, was condemned by the Holy Office in a manner that caused a great disturbance. I met him personally for the first time at a moral theology conference in Luxemburg in 1952. During a long walk he related to me his difficult fate after the Russian occupation of his home town Breslau, his imprisonment by the Russians, his adventure-filled flight to the West, the complete loss of his not insignificant paternal heritage. Nevertheless, he felt all this suffering as nothing in comparison to what had been visited upon him by the Holy Office, especially through Father Hürth. When after the war he applied for the professorial chair in Münster, Father Hürth did everything possible to prevent it. I was his guest in the following years in Münster and learned to wonder all the more at his unshakable love for the Church. The Council justified him completely.

Just as with Herbert Doms, Bernardin Krempel's book *Die Zweckfrage der Ehe in neuer Beleuchtung* (*The Question of the Purpose of Marriage in a New Light*, 1941) was placed on the Index of Forbidden Books. The manner in which I came into contact with Krempel was not a pleasant one for me. Krempel complained (with right) that in the first edition of my book *The Law of Christ* (1954) I did not do justice to the goals of his book. There developed a several-year-long friendly exchange of letters which acquainted me with his deep suffering of soul. Krempel had been literally excluded like a leper. When he wished to defend himself in Rome he was received neither by the

Holy Office nor by Father Hürth. His Order likewise played along with this tragedy. Thus it happened that he found consolation in the friendship of a noble woman, and finally married her civilly. However, without having consummated the marriage, they separated again in mutual understanding in order once again to be admitted to the sacraments. The persistent effort of friends finally obtained from Rome the lifting of his suspensions. Later he taught philosophy at Königstein.

Krempel died shortly before the beginning of the Council. The nuns in whose hospital he died related movingly of his holy death: "We have never seen anyone die so gifted by God." During a pause in our work in the preconciliar subcommission on marriage I related this to Father Tromp and Father Hürth, without remarking that I knew anything about the disturbing relationship with Hürth. Tears rolled down the face of Hürth; they reconciled me with him.

I also shared inwardly in the suffering of soul of my Dutch confrere Father W. Duynstee, a highly thought of professor of the history of law at the Catholic University of Nijmegen, and author of the modest book *The Sixth Commandment in Modern Life* (1935). A well known woman psychological therapist with whom he worked together in pastoral work was converted by him. During a canonical visitation in Holland by Father Tromp he was suddenly struck by his lightning: he was banned from Holland without his or his superiors' being given a concrete reason. He lived out his exile for many years in Sant'Alfonso during the first period of my Roman stay. Tromp never once spoke with Duynstee himself. So far as we could learn he had asked a number of male patients of the woman psychological therapist who were being pastorally cared for by Duynstee whether the priest had clearly said to them that masturbation was a mortal sin. Without any understanding of the matter, they denied that he had. Outside of myself and the Father General, no one in the house knew what the reason for his presence was. He worked humbly in Sant'Alfonso in the library and archives. One can truly say that he was a saintly man. It was only in the preparatory period before the Council that Cardinal Alfrink and the Father General were able to gain permission for him to visit Holland (however, not Nijmegen!), and later to return home. I can well remember how he asked me whether the continued exile from Nijmegen could have any purpose other than to save the face of the Holy Office.

A similar case was the banning of Father Kentenich, the founder of the Schönstatt Movement and a flourishing congregation of sisters. Father Tromp had banned him to America with the strict order to have no contact with his foundation. He obeyed in model fashion. During the Council Bishop Tenhumberg of Münster asked me to evaluate the writings and manuscripts of Father Kentenich and to write a judgment for Pope Paul VI. I did so. I am truthfully able to say that I did not discover the least thing which could look like heresy. Paul VI ordered the complete rehabilitation of Kentenich. The manner in which it took place once again gave me very much to think about.

In what way did you share the experience of the attack of Monsignors Piolanti and Romeo of the Lateran University against the Biblical Institute?

I in fact did share the experience very closely. The opening salvo was an essay of Cardinal Ruffini's from Palermo in the *Osservatore Romano* soon after the death of Pius XII in which the decisive teaching of the encyclical *Divino afflante Spiritu* on the study of the Holy Scriptures was attacked as nonsense. It was already clear that the target was the Biblical Institute and especially Augustin Bea, who had played a decisive role in the writing of that significant encyclical. Piolanti, the Rector of the Lateran University, a "pillar of the Holy Office" in questions of dogma and biblical exegesis, spoke before his students of his own plans to set up at his university a biblical institute against "the Jesuits." Several students reported this to me. There followed the aggressive article of his friend and fellow fighter Monsignor Antonio Romeo, "The Encyclical *Divino afflante Spiritu* and New Opinions" in the journal edited by the Lateran, *Divinitas* (1960, pp. 387–456): a classic example of "rabies theologorum," of theologians foaming at the mouth. Shortly thereafter the two most beloved and respected professors of the Biblical Institute, Stanislaus Lyonnet and Maximillian Zerwick, received a formal teaching prohibition.

At that time I was teaching about 200 seminarians at the Pastoral Institute of the Lateran University. They asked me before my lecture for my judgment. During the lecture I did not say a word about it, but at the end I said in the prayer "Oremus: A furore theologorum," and all answered in chorus: "Libera nos Domine!" Piolanti was angry about this, but he could do nothing to me since he knew that Pope John XXIII was well disposed toward me.

It is still a puzzle to me today why Pope John allowed the Holy Office to carry out this dark affair. By the time of his death the teaching prohibition against the two professors was still not lifted. Did he not want to trigger a challenge of the Holy Office against himself by a decisive word? Often in history popes, with the best of will, were powerless.

In 1964 I said to Paul VI: "The fact that this teaching prohibition still persists is a scandal not only for the Roman

Catholic Church but for all Christianity." To this he responded: "I am sorry that I have not yet found the time to concern myself with this matter in a thoroughgoing way." After a deep breath I dared say: "But you surely could give the matter over to Father Bea or the Superior General of the Jesuits. They can review the whole situation." After a couple of days the whole matter was taken care of. The Pope had laid the matter in the hands of Father Bea. In his following visit to the Lateran University Paul VI spoke with great clarity about this senseless, intolerant struggle and closed with the words: "Mai più"—"never again!" Several years later Father Lyonnet was named a Consultor to the Holy Office. His burial just a few years ago was a triumphal procession of a saint. Many of those who knew him revered him as such.

Whoever is convinced that a therapeutic treatment of the "structures of sin" is possible and necessary should study this case in detail, and indeed with the categories of the sociology of knowledge which has thoroughly investigated the conflict between the knowledge of salvation and the knowledge of dominance (for example, Max Scheler). This is certainly not done in order to narrow the authority of the Pope. On the contrary, it is done for the sake of a fundamental reform in the sense of collegiality (synodal constitution) and subsidiarity, in order to protect and strengthen the true authority of the Pope.

Is it true that the Holy Office, even during and immediately after the Council, gave free reign to their hostile attitude toward the well-known theologians who had contributed much to the success of the Council?

Note that, aside from the indisputable fact that the most influential Council theologians in the preparatory commissions and even in the conciliar commissions did not have it easy, there is indeed a great deal of proof that the Holy Office never ceased to suspect them. An example known throughout the world is the difficulties which Karl Rahner had. The Holy Office even demanded that he no longer be allowed to publish anything without submitting it first to the censorship of that office. It was thanks only to the brave intervention of the German-speaking cardinals and the decisiveness of John XXIII that this was finally prevented. I received from a bishop a photocopy of an official letter from Cardinal Parente in which he named me among the untrustworthy theologians. Of all of the documentation which I have, probably the most impressive is a letter from the Assessor of the Holy Office to my friend Giovanni Rossi, dated February 24, 1964. This letter, of which I immediately received a photocopy through my friend, is an impressive proof of the Curial opposition to the Pope. Henri Fesquet, a world-known journalist of the Council, wrote in his diary notes of the Council on October 29, 1963: "The Pope had emphasized anew in his private audiences: Father Congar is one of the theologians who has contributed most to the preparation of the Council and whose thoughts are most appreciated by the Council Fathers." Soon thereafter the Pope spoke similarly in a public audience.

Nevertheless, on February 24, 1964, Parente wrote to Giovanni Rossi of the *Pro Civitate Christiani* (Assisi): "The Cardinal's secretary has directed me to inform you that, to say the least, it is not wise to publish in *Rocca* hymns of praise of theologians like Father Congar, who through their publications, despite their genius and learnedness, have given occasions of ambiguity and reserve. A magazine which finds its way into the hands of all sorts of people and of so many Christian families must, particularly in matters of doctrine and lines of theological reflection, hold itself to a more certain line. . . . His Eminence expects that you will avoid such incidents" [the full text is in the Italian edition of this book].

When Paul VI had praised Yves Congar in a public audience, the latter revealed to me that thereupon a more comfortable room was provided him in the Dominican convent. These and other similar cases gave me a foretaste of what could await us when the Council Fathers again went home. I saw on many occasions how the resistant will of the men of the Curia who were not open to reform was directed against the Dutch bishops and their advisors. The number of Dutch-speaking bishops at the Council was considerable, due to the fact that the relatively small number of Dutch Catholics had sent more priests to the mission churches than the populous church of Italy had. I was quite certain that the extremely gifted and at the same time modest Father Edward Schillebeeckx would soon become a target. And thus it happened. A whole book could be written about this. Schillebeeckx did not let himself be led astray, but his health suffered considerably during this ordeal.

Did you observe the obstructive attitude of the Curia and especially of the Doctrinal Congregation toward the Latin American theologians?

Certainly, a number of these liberation theologians were earlier students of mine at the Academia Alfonsiana and remained close to me in friendship. Through them I also came into contact with Gustavo Gutiérrez. I obtained a copy of the document of charges directed against him by the Doctrinal Congregation along with carefully composed analyses of it, for example, by the (ecumenical) theo-

logical faculty of Berkeley, California. That is the most
shameful example of the complete harmony between ignorance and arrogance, to use once again this well-known
phrase of Cardinal Pellegrino. The superficiality with
which sentences were torn out of their context and quota-
tions were being attributed to the authors bordered on the
unbelievable. In Gutiérrez's case the charge of Marxism
and the instigation of violent revolution is most especially
and absolutely unfounded. I have seldom read anywhere
such convincing arguments in favor of a nonviolent solution as by my friend Gutiérrez.

Concerning the charge of Marxism there is a special
circumstance which I would now like to turn to here in
more detail. When as a young student I read the major
work of Karl Marx, *Capital,* I discovered with outrage how
much proof Marx brought to document his thesis that religion is nothing other than opium for the people, that is, a
propping up of a false consciousness in the mind of the
exploited. I was deeply shaken. The liberation theologians
experienced exactly the same thing when they studied the
history of the colonization-missionization of Latin America in an unbiased way. We discover a "religion" which
misdirects the knowledge of salvation to the service of
"the knowledge of domination," and thus fundamentally
falsifies it. We can do nothing other than *likewise* thoroughly research the history of Europe and especially of
the Church in this light.

And yet, in the end that has nothing to do with Marxism as such. For Marx sees this misuse of religion as an
"iron law of dialectical materialism." We on the contrary
say openly that it is one of the most devilish temptations
and sins against God and humanity that has the severest
consequences. These sins and the resultant "structures of
sins" must be disclosed so that we and the Church can be

liberated from them. From the perspective of liberation theology, thus and only thus do we believe that one can overcome the Marxian fundamental thesis. We see on the contrary pure apologetics as a sinful cover-up maneuver that gives the advantage to Marxism and severely disadvantages the Church. We therefore need not wonder that "church leaders" and church groups which are in league with the powerholders and oppressors, who are linked together with the militarists and the wealthy, instinctively sense that they thereby really are sitting among the accused. Without the will to repent, they simply do not wish to perceive. The category which most of all is plagued by such insidious temptations includes those who crave and hunt after churchly honors. All too easily they develop a numbed conscience. From there the bitter animosity toward liberation theology arises. Other churchmen fall in with this not because of a diseased conscience but simply because they know nothing of the categories of the sociology of knowledge.

Gustavo Gutiérrez was not so shaken by the chess tactics of the Vatican in trying to make the episcopacy of Peru the "cat's paw" to condemn his theology—which did not succeed—as he was upset by the whole style and method of the accusatory document with which the Doctrinal Congregation initiated the doctrinal trial against him. On the afternoon before his first summons he was with me in my room at Sant'Alfonso. We prayed long together, not only for us, but especially for the Church. I could not admire Gustavo more. This first great theologian from the native population of Peru had done his studies from a wheelchair. He is physically severely handicapped but has an iron will for action. Along with his studies he spent a great deal of time in the pastoral care of the poorest people. How tightly closed must the minds of those men behind the scenes be that they cannot grasp the great respect this Indio is worthy of. With the help of his friends and especially thanks to the wisdom of the majority of the Peruvian bishops, the Gutiérrez affair went well in Rome. About that also much more could be said.

The Boff affair became more known worldwide than the Gutiérrez affair because the latter led to no disciplining. The Boff case was unique insofar as two of the most respected cardinals of the Church accompanied him to Rome and argued for him. The command of silence laid upon him was a widely discussed event. He showed himself obedient, but in no way as servile.

The case of Charles Curran drew great attention and it was known to the press that you accompanied him as a kind of defender to a decisive meeting with the Doctrinal Congregation. Could you say something to us about that?

More than twenty-five years ago Curran was a student with us at the Academia Alfonsiana, and he wrote a doctoral dissertation on the respect to be shown an erring conscience according to St. Alphonsus. Already at that time he drew attention to himself by his extraordinary ability, not least because he was one of the few Americans who spoke fluent Latin. He is a deeply faithful and devout theologian and a friend of the poor. His income is for their benefit. He cherishes a simple lifestyle and values being with others. It is no wonder that for many students of the Catholic University in Washington, and beyond, he was known as the ideal theologian.

Without realizing it, in some way I shared responsibility for his being caught up in a turmoil in Washington. The story began thus. After the first Council session students and professors invited three outstanding Council theologians to lecture at the Catholic University in Washington. The conservative rector of the university, a bishop, prevented their coming to the university, causing a great uproar. The professors demanded a sign of reparation and so brought me into the situation by requesting that the chair for moral theology, which had become open, should be offered to me. When I declined it I was asked for a suggestion, and my suggestion was Charles Curran. He quickly became popular, partly because of his human qualities. But both the conservative chancellor and the rector wanted to be rid of him and did not renew his contract, though they gave no reason. A strike by the professors and students was almost one hundred percent successful and forced the leadership not only to reinstate but to promote him. In 1968, along with many colleagues from America, he signed a declaration about *Humanae vitae*, according to which there can be situations in which married people may with a good conscience use artificial means of contraception. He was never forgiven for that by some. In 1979 (I already had cancer of the throat then) he showed me the letter of the Doctrinal Congregation which had opened a doctrinal trial against him. He was obviously stunned by this. He lived, as so many others, in the conviction that a doctrinal trial was possible only in the case of a violation of a teaching of the faith.

In his correspondence which ran through 1986 he could never learn whether there was a defender for him at the Doctrinal Congregation. Likewise, his repeated inquiries as to whether all dissent against definitely non-infallible doctrines was punishable, remained without an answer. Only toward the end was this confirmed to him. It is indeed, among other things, also in the new Canon Law that dissent regarding non-infallible teachings is punishable. His case exclusively concerned questions of sexual ethics, as is, to my knowledge, almost always so in the many cases against moral theologians. In the Curran case it dealt with borderline questions involving masturbation, contraception, sexual relations of engaged couples before the formal holding of the marriage ceremony, pastoral counseling for homosexuals, and pastoral counseling for the divorced.

Are you personally exactly of the same opinion as Charles Curran in all of these matters?

By no means! In questions of sexual morality I indeed am known as pastorally kind but theologically rather conservative. In many questions I am more reserved than Curran, simply because I have not come to a clear judgment. However, Curran, according to the opinion of most who know him and his writings, in general follows a moderate middle line. He is definitely not contaminated by the *Zeitgeist* or the counter-culture of sexual consumerism. He believes firmly in the meaning of priestly celibacy when this is chosen out of conviction. He has, in many individual questions, tested carefully how far pastoral solutions and pastoral counseling can go forward to meet men and women in difficulties. Only the future will show whether he perhaps had gone somewhat too far in some points. Likewise, he has never maintained that his suggestions or hypotheses, as they are formulated, should be simply translated into practice contrary to expressed doctrines of the Magisterium. The points in which he has contradicted the Doctrinal Congregation with an iron firmness are the right and under certain circumstances also the obligation to express dissent regarding non-infallible doctrines and the meaning of academic freedom, which is bound together with that right of appropriate dissent. He has always emphasized that his dissent is located within a comprehensive consent.

How did the "dialogue" with the Doctrinal Congregation to which you accompanied Charles Curran on March 8, 1986, go?

The dean of the theological faculty of the Catholic University in Washington (Fr. William Cenkner), a Dominican theologian, and Monsignor George Higgins, one of the most respected priests in America and the former secretary of the American Bishops' Conference, accompanied us to the waiting room. Since Cardinal Ratzinger was not yet free, we used the time for spontaneous common prayer. Just before the cardinal came in, one of the four of us had prayed, "May God stand by us that we may be concerned not so much about our victory as about the kingdom of God."

Shortly before, the cardinal was handed a letter from the bishop of Curran's home diocese in which the bishop described his priest as an outstanding example of the priestly spirit with a sense of responsibility as a theologian. To our surprise the cardinal said to us that this letter could not change the situation since the judgment had already been made. Thereupon we asked the question: "What then was the purpose of the invitation to a colloquium?" After several subterfuges the cardinal granted that there was still a small possibility that the whole matter could be thought over again once more.

Thereupon I made my plea. The Doctrinal Congregation should reflect that when it concerns a charge of dissent, this institution and especially its predecessors stand before the bar of history because of a multiplicity of longlasting dissents against the overwhelming majority of theologians and faithful. I named several known examples. The men of the Doctrinal Congregation were indeed impressed with my candor, but whether this weighty argument could correspondingly move them to any rethinking of the matter escapes my knowledge. One would like to hope so, even in the face of the fact that in the new Code of Canon Law dissent as such turns up as a punishable act, even without a previous discussion in the appropriate commissions, and indeed in all questions which deal with non-infallible teachings of the church—all historical experiences notwithstanding.

Then we discussed matters in a good, humane climate, in my judgment. At a critical point Curran, however, asked something, somewhat upset: "Why am I being singled out as a scapegoat when I do not belong to the group of extreme theologians?" The question was not answered. I put in a remark: "I can only hope that in the end Cardinal Ratzinger will not be made a scapegoat for many matters."

Then we spoke very candidly about the suggestion which Curran earlier, through Cardinal Bernardin and Archbishop Hickey (the chancellor of the Catholic University of America), had made. Curran offered in the future to give no courses and no seminars at the Catholic University on questions of sexual ethics. However, he should be allowed to teach in the other areas of morals and social ethics, that is, on matters in which there never had been accusations against him. In addition, it had already been more than ten years since he had given any lectures or seminars on sexual ethics.

In the end I had the impression that Cardinal Ratzinger was prepared to bring this suggestion with his recommendation to the next session of the Doctrinal Congregation. With this a very sensible compromise would have been arranged. Curran was not so optimistic. Unfortunately, further developments showed that his worry was justified. I presume that there were forces in America itself among the powerful churchmen who wanted to have Curran censured. Over 750 doctors of theology and canon law had signed a petition asking that Rome forego all disciplining—in vain.

Soon thereafter came the disciplining of Seattle's Bishop Hunthausen, who is very close to his people, and who had become a thorn in the side of conservative politics in America due to his involvement in the peace movement. The relation of progressive Catholics to the Vatican was severely shaken through the simultaneous occurrence of these two cases, while the traditionalists were overjoyed. An intensification of the already existing polarization was the high price paid. Curran received invitations to take over professorial chairs from the most famous universities in America. But he gave himself time. In autumn of the same year he came to me in Gars for a spiritual retreat. I heard not a single complaining word against any person from his mouth. He is determined to struggle for the principle, but absolutely without any violence. In late 1990, Curran accepted a permanent chair of theology at Southern Methodist University in Texas.

Outside of Charles Curran, have any other of your former students had difficulty with the Vatican?

In the past thirty-five years I have had over 3,000 students in Rome who specialized in moral or pastoral theology. A great number were, so to speak, silently withdrawn from traffic and shoved off onto a side track insofar as bishops obediently followed up on a signal from the Vatican. One of the most gifted speakers and writers was transferred to a small parish after a *monitum* from Rome. He accepted it without protest. Since precisely at that time a large paternal heritage fell to him, he transformed it into a rehabilitation center for drug addicts. He has a persuasive personality and great healing powers. He recently related to me that his bishop asked him in the most friendly manner why he no longer published anything nor held any lectures. I wanted to know how he reacted. He said: "I smiled at the bishop, and he understood."

The case of my very gifted former student, the Claretian Father Forcano, caused a great sensation in the Spanish press. He was a highly respected editor of the widely read journal *Mission Abierta* and had undergone a long-lasting doctrinal trial, above all because of his book *New Sexual Morality*. The document charging him was almost as superficial and unobjective as in the case of Gutiérrez. In the end it was demanded, in view of the charges against him, that before he published the revised text he should submit it to the censor of the Doctrinal Congregation. His superior and I, who had read the improved text, were impressed with the self-denial of Father Forcano. Nevertheless, he decided to let a quotation from the declaration of the French bishops concerning the solution of conflict cases regarding the norms of *Humanae vitae*, no. 14, stand. Obviously, they were very angry about this.

The verdict, which his Superior General was supposed to carry out, and finally under pressure did carry out personally, was much more severe than in the case of Curran: removal as editor, no further collaboration with *Mission Abierta*, no further publication without permission by the Doctrinal Congregation. Still, his faith is not shaken, although inwardly he suffered a much more severe shock than did Curran.

Until now you have spoken of your deep concern in view of the difficulties of others. Could you also tell us something of your own severe and long-lasting doctrinal trial?

When, as a young professor, I came to Rome I heard an experienced General Consultor, a Flem, say that the strongest proof that we Redemptorists have not done much for the renewal of theology is the fact that none of us has yet landed on the Index of Forbidden Books. It appears to be almost something like a "rule" that theologians who in any way perform a pioneer work get involved with the highest Church bureau of control. Only the most tiresome camp follower will remain unenlightened by this. This has to do with a long tradition, which is represented by the name "Inquisition," which—although it must be admitted that in general the Roman Inquisition was not as severe as the Spanish Inquisition—was linked together with a system of domination that was interested in uniformity.

Before I relate my negative experiences, I would not like to skip mentioning that I have found much love and recognition in the Vatican, first of all by popes, but then also by many highly placed and not so highly placed persons. I admonish the reader not to be misled into too quick generalizations. Even today I have good friends in the Vatican. Even there, there are open and absolutely selfless men. I would gladly add "and women," but for women the Vatican has hardly been a place of much influence thus far. This does not foster a healthy "climate," and here lies one of the points in which the Vatican is not representative of the world Church.

Earlier I mentioned that in the midst of the Council my fatherly friend Cardinal Cento often warned me to be alert against machinations which aimed at eliminating my influence. They came, from what I can see, almost exclusively from the "Palace of the Holy Office." I can of course understand this just from the fact that of the seventy documents, which were prepared for the Council under the influence of this bureau, none had a chance of being accepted. The commission which prepared the schema for liturgical reform was oriented completely differently. Cardinal Lercaro and his closest collaborator Bugnini, with whom I was already well acquainted from my first visit to Rome, stood highest of all on the blacklists after the Council. That the Curia was able to issue a censure was one of the first signs of alarm.

Soon after Cardinal Cento had again warned me, I was summoned by the Assessor of the Holy Office, Archbishop Pietro Parente. He said to me in a domineering manner: "You have said in America that one does not have to listen to the Magisterium of the Pope." There then followed a full-blown dressing down.

I answered him finally: "I first of all want to remark that I know of the direction of the Pope that one should hear me out in the Holy Office before bringing charges against me. Now, however, you have not heard me out before you addressed this reprimand to me. Secondly, I may say that I am in fact more clever than you think. I have known that you have spied upon me with the help of the Apostolic Delegate Vagnozzi. Therefore, during my stay in America I have always had a confrere with me who recorded on tape everything which I said before large or small circles. The tapes are at your disposal. About a course on the sacrament of penance which you have mentioned, there is already available an exact transcription of the tapes."

His answer: "Give us the material." I did so immediately. After many months no reaction was forthcoming, so I called Archbishop Parente. Only his secretary came to the telephone, asking me what I wanted to know. As I spoke of the material which I had handed over for investigation, he said to me: "That is already all taken care of. We have been very much astonished at your wisdom and balance." The matter was not spoken of again. What is indicative, however, is that there also was never any apology.

Later, I was summoned again by Archbishop Parente, as always, by telephone. He chided me that I had intervened with the Pope and other persons in favor of a bishop reprimanded by the Holy Office. "There is no recourse beyond the Supreme." Supreme, the "highest of all," was the beloved abbreviation for the "Suprema Sacra Congregatio. . . ." He closed his speech with the tip: "If you continue to do this, there will be no career for you."

At that, I went on the counter-attack with the question: "Do you mean that in the sense of the Skinnerian mixture of reward and punishment, promise and threat, or is it an acknowledgement that I serve the Church not for the sake of reward?" His answer: "It is an expression of admiration!" Did I perhaps "seduce him" into a lie or a dissemblance, I asked myself afterwards. But Parente could simply not have answered my question.

Undoubtedly, the most significant summons from Parente took place between the close of the work of the Commission on Population Problems and *Humanae vitae*. In an interview the journalist of the magazine *La Rocca* asked me among other things what position I expected from Pope Paul VI on the norm of *Casti connubii*. I had answered that at this moment I did not wish to speak on the matter, but that I was absolutely confident that Pope Paul VI would not contradict the Council. Parente screamed at me: "With that you have denied the superior-

ity of the Pope over the Council!" I retorted: "To maintain
the coherence of the Pope with the Council promulgated
by the Pope himself and to deny his superiority over the
Council are two completely different things. In any case,
tell me now what your purpose is!"

At the last summons by Parente I was most firmly determined. I showed Parente the three written documents
which compromised him, among which were the afore-
mentioned letter to Don Giovanni Rossi against Congar,
and one against me, which had the official seal. I asked
him, "Do you want me to publish these documents?" He
wanted to grab them, but I took them back quickly. Still he
persisted: "How did you get these documents?" I explained to him that although I did not have at my disposal a
network of spies, these things simply flew to me. Then I
repeated my question. Parente went chalk-white and had
to sit down immediately. I feared a stroke and began to
calm him, saying that I was not interested in going public
with these things, but rather simply wished to put an end
to this nonsense. He assured me that he understood and
that at an appropriate occasion he would speak publicly in
favor of this theologian. He kept his promise, and for many
long years I had a respite from the Holy Office.

*Did it ever go beyond verbal expressions? Did you ever
receive any written documents?*

I found in my archives only one, an official written
inquiry from Cardinal Ottaviani to me while I was in the
United States. It concerned a newspaper report, according
to which I had advised the pastors and leading persons of
the Christian Family Movement to respect the consciences of penitents and those seeking advice on questions of birth control. I had referred in this to citations

from St. Alphonsus, and not at all to the expected results of the Papal Commission. I explained this in my written answer and was not pressured further. This letter from Cardinal Ottaviani was dated February 8, 1967.

On June 26 Parente was made a cardinal. Monsignor Philippe took his place as the second man in the Holy Office, as Jerome Hamer did later.

Ottaviani retired from his post on August 1, 1968. His successor was the Archbishop of Zagreb, Cardinal Seper. I had been on the best of terms during the Council with Seper and Philippe.

When and how did matters evolve to a doctrinal trial against you?

On June 4, 1975, the gathering of the cardinals of the Doctrinal Congregation determined to initiate a doctrinal trial against me, specifically and mainly because of my book *Medical Ethics*. On June 13, Paul VI approved this decision. [Editor's note: The text in question is *Etica Medica*, Rome: Editione Paolini, 1972. The fourth edition was published in 1975; page references are to that edition. The work was originally published under the title *Hellender Dienst: Etische Probleme der Modernen Medizin*, Mainz: Matthias-Grunewald, 1972. An English version of the second edition was published in 1973 as *Medical Ethics*, Notre Dame: Fides/London: Society of St. Paul Publications.]

The official documents were sent to me altogether through my Superior General, Father Joseph Pfab, who had been my student in moral theology and canon law at Gars. I insert here only the documents directed against me personally. I believe they need no detailed commentary. They speak for themselves. The first document of the

Doctrinal Congregation (December 16, 1975) I will pass over and begin with my response of February 5, 1976, in which I go into all of the points charged against me.

(Document 1)
To His Eminence
Cardinal Franjo Seper
Prefect of the Doctrinal Congregation
                    Rome, February 5, 1976

Your Eminence,
    Shortly after my return on February 1, your letter with the date of December 16, 1975, was handed to me by my Superior General.
    Allow me to answer with complete openness. You will understand that I will read this document of the Doctrinal Congregation in connection with an unusually sharp article of the *Osservatore Romano* at the beginning of the Holy Year of Reconciliation. The article climaxed at that time in the charge that I wish to undermine the Magisterium of the Pope. That is also the central charge in your document. The proof for such a charge was not brought forth by the Vatican paper. Moreover no one thought it necessary to ask me whether the alleged interview really was given by me. Many highly placed persons of the Catholic world have personally expressed to me their astonishment at the content and tone of that article and at the same time their sympathy for me as the one attacked. You will see from my analysis of your document why I put these two things together, along with several earlier experiences.
    The document of the Doctrinal Congrega-

tion will interest the writer of history. The manner in which the accusations are raised and the way in which texts of the accused are analyzed may well be unusual even in the long history of the Doctrinal Congregation and its predecessors. The clarification of this matter may be providential for the Church. I respond to each point:

1. After a very general inquiry the accusation is raised: "In fact the contribution of revelation is minimalized and almost entirely emptied out (cf. p. 29)." My response: In view of the especially careful working out of the specifically Christian view of the physician's ethics, the translator and publisher of the French edition chose the title: "Perspective chrétienne pour une médicine humaine" ("A Christian View of Human Medicine," Paris: Fayard, 1973). Whoever reads pages 29–34 carefully will see how stringent the demands are that are made on a specifically Christian morality. There can be absolutely no question here of an emptying out. According to the document of the Doctrinal Congregation addressed to me, what here is at issue are questions of *fundamental theology*. Clearly "proof texts" for individual theses cannot be sought for here. Compare, please, pages 113–119, 199–207, 251–274. While the pages to which your document refers work out the general fundamental lines of a specifically Christian ethics, the pages given by me here lead the discussion further into a relationship with the meaning of life, of death, of illness and healing, and always expressly within the perspective of revelation, especially within the perspective of the word of God.

The charge leaves me speechless. I ask the Doctrinal Congregation to name me any traditional text of Catholic ethics for the physician in which these goals are treated with such care, in so many pages, and with such stringent demand.

A general accusation charges incompleteness and inadequacy. Was that ever in the past a basis for a trial? In this regard could not every author, and indeed the publications of the Doctrinal Office, be brought to trial?

My honest purpose was to show according to *Optatam totius* of the Second Vatican Council how the whole view of morality must be nourished by the word of God. Neither the number of pages which are devoted to this concern nor the degree of the demand on conscience provides a basis for the accusation of an "emptying out" ("svuotare"). Still worse was the exaggeration: "Quasi completamente svuotato," "almost completely emptied out."

The generalized accusation about inadequacy should not be raised in view of the fact that until now no author has so completely worked out an ethics for physicians from a specifically Christian perspective.

2. It is further claimed: "On the other hand the theme of the natural moral law (pp. 78–87) is treated in a way that severely lacks depth. Cannot this charge be raised against many traditionalistic authors? Why then the charge precisely against me? I have in so many publications attempted to present a specifically Christian view of the natural law of morality that I do not once again have to say everything. I limited myself to

those points which are important for the dialogue with health care professionals. Precisely here it is necessary to eliminate misunderstandings which have almost entirely prevented dialogue. The evaluator has obviously not paid attention to what the purpose of this book is: the evangelization of the contemporary world, starting points for the dialogue, the working out of a truly Christian attitude.

3. My interpretation of the natural moral law is challenged particularly on one point, namely, my criticisms of a sentence of St. Thomas; otherwise I have spoken about him in a very laudatory manner. Allow me to cite the text of Thomas which I criticized: "There is in human beings an inclination to certain things flowing from nature which they share with the rest of living beings (*animalia*): and correspondingly they belong to the natural law which through nature teaches all living beings (*animalia*), as, for example, the union of man and woman and the bringing up of progeny and similar things" (*Summa theologica*, Ia IIae q.94, a.2).

May I here ask the Doctrinal Congregation how this text ought to be interpreted? A great number of theologians and anthropologists emphasize as I do the specifically human character of human sexuality and sexual morality, and share in my criticism of that text. The love of the Church and the service of healing oblige us to eliminate every defective statement and interpretation which can place the credibility of our proclamation in question.

4. The further accusation is raised: "Con-

nected with this methodological confusion is found an ambiguous use of the category, the signs of the times: a truly ambiguous manner of speaking."

This is an interesting point, for on page 63 I in no way speak of the "signs of the times," (*Zeichen der Zeit*) but rather of the *Zeitgeist*. I used this German word, with which every educated Italian is familiar, but I also have in addition clearly translated it. I first speak of the "positive elements of the contemporary *Zeitgeist*"; and then "of an intensification of moral conviction" (p. 64), all in view of the working out of a codex for physicians by the body of physicians themselves. Whoever reads the chapter attentively will immediately see that there is no question of the "signs of the times" in the theological sense, but rather of the *Zeitgeist*. Whoever possesses an average schooling knows what this expression in the intellectual life of Germany, France, and beyond means.

Here a decisive question must be posed: Was this document of indictment checked over by no one? Was no one assigned to carefully check the indictment to see whether or not it dealt justly with the aims of the indicted author? This is a very weighty question for me and for many. It is unthinkable that two persons independent of each other could confuse *Zeitgeist* and the "signs of the times" (*Zeichen der Zeit*).

Now to the charge on page 30. It collapses in that it is connected with the basic misunderstanding of page 63. Nevertheless, I will answer it directly in order to show that I take the Doctrinal

Congregation seriously even under such circumstances. The Second Vatican Council speaks of the signs of the times as signs of the presence of God (cf. *Gaudium et spes*). The document distributed by an official organ of the Vatican to the bishops in preparation for the bishops' synod of 1974 (outline of the discussion, part 2, II/F) states that the signs of the times are to be generally understood as *locus theologicus*. And the *Instrumentum laboris* for the same synod emphasized further that evangelization must pay attention to how God reveals his will through the signs of the times (e.g., N. 22 and 46). That is precisely how I understand an ongoing self-revelation of the will of God in salvation history. I have in my works often indicated that the signs of the time can be understood only within the perspective of the revelation in Jesus Christ. In this connection may I refer to my book *Morale ed evangelizzazione del mondo di oggi* (Rome: Ed. Paoline, 1974, pp. 9–39; *Evangelization Today*, Notre Dame: Fides, 1974).

I synthesized my manner of seeing the continued work of God thus: "Christ is the decisive and final word which the Father speaks to humanity. No progress in science and technology, no knowledge of history will ever be able to surpass Christ or set him in the second place. He is, in his love for the Father and for humanity, in what he has done in his earthly life through to his resurrection, the key to salvation for all time and the truth against which all partial truths finally must be measured. However, the unfolding of the history of the world and the Church through the millen-

nia can and should contribute to an awakening of
the knowledge of Christ through its works and its
progress in history. Christ does not become
greater through ongoing history, but our knowledge of the plan of salvation which is revealed to
the world in Christ does become more complete
and close to life in our heart through the working
of the Spirit in the history of the Church
and above all in the saints" (Bernhard Häring,
"Wie als Christ handeln?" J. Hüttenbügel, ed.,
Gott, Mensch, Universum [Graz-Vienna-Cologne,
1974], pp. 632–33).

The working of God is always in his Word.
And therefore we must listen for this Word. It is
precisely that which is meant when I speak as in
the official Vatican document of the signs of the
time as *locus theologicus*.

5. The next, likewise unargued, accusation
speaks of a "falling into an ethical relativism
which derives the criteria of a virtuous act exclusively from the historical situation." As I read this
charge a strong feeling of disgust came over me.
How should I disprove this extremely serious
charge since there is not a single item of argumentation given for it? This charge weighs all the
more heavily since the Doctrinal Congregation
presumably is familiar with the rest of my works.
From them there is more than enough to show
how constantly I have turned my efforts against
the charge of historicism, which is made against
me here. If I have done this with greater nuance
than those theologians who have neglected the
historical context of the language and the ethical
statements, then I may be seen as having made a

significant contribution in this regard so that it is inconceivable that I should be accused of having contributed to the promotion of historicism, of relativism. Has it occurred to no one in your Congregation how weighty the word "unicamente" (exclusively) weighs? May I request that you personally read my book *Medical Ethics* itself so that you may realize the enormous injustice of this accusation. You will find a brief synthesis of my thought on this question in the already referred to essay in *Gott, Mensch, Universum*, pages 640–647, under the heading "The Formation of Specifically Christian Norms."

6. The key to the entire construction of the case against me is in the following accusation: "Thus one finally denies the jurisdiction of the Magisterium in moral questions" (p. 68). What I say on page 68 is fundamentally nothing other than what Pope John XXIII in his opening address at the Second Vatican Council had said. I maintain only that a healthy hermeneutics is needed in order to do justice to the documents of the ecclesial Magisterium and to find light in them for completely new problems. This same view is found, incidentally, also in *Mysterium Ecclesiae*, published by the Doctrinal Congregation. The accusation which refers to page 68 would be justified then only if one were to look at the statements of the Magisterium on moral questions as timeless and not in need of a hermeneutic.

As with the question of the incredible misunderstanding in regard to *Zeitgeist*, the pressing question comes up again here: Was no one in the Doctrinal Congregation assigned to check carefully whether in the indictment the author had been dealt with justly? This question comes up here inexorably since the Holy Father himself is involved in this matter and hence precisely such an accusation will be especially effective in destroying me in his heart and in his eyes. This is the fourth time, known to me, wherein the Holy Father is involved in similar summary accusations against me. These seriously endanger the ministry of the Holy Father and the Curia to mediate salvation. How in such circumstances can men and women recognize the Roman Church as the "leader of the covenant of love"? I know very well how much the Holy Father himself endeavors to give this witness of love.

I am not saying that all of the four cases known to me of similar accusations against my person were at the initiative of the Doctrinal Congregation. An identical accusation came as early as the time of the Council from the Holy Office. At that time I could show on the basis of the transcript from tapes, that I had never uttered the statements that had been placed in my mouth. Fortunately all my lectures from that year were recorded on tape. The tapes prove how respectfully and emphatically I spoke of the person and the office of the Pope. Nevertheless, an apology never was sent me. And I do not know whether the Holy Father was ever informed of the true state of affairs.

In this case, even the page in question (68) proves, as do all my writings, that I take the Magisterium of the Pope very seriously. Many never express a criticism against the Curia because they no longer take it seriously. Such an accusation will never be raised against me. In the analytic index in my *Medical Ethics* (*Etica medica*, 4th ed., 1975, p. 407) you will find the references to the pages which refer to the Magisterium. Thus you can, if you wish, orient yourself quickly and see what unjust accusations against me are borne to the Holy Father.

I acknowledge that until now I have allowed these accusations to pile up in order to find more time for prayer and service of the Gospel. However, I see that my own service in the Church and the well-being of the Church now absolutely demand a clarification. I must be certain that the Holy Father is finally and clearly informed about the injustice of all these accusations. I therefore request Your Eminence to arrange an audience for me with the Holy Father. At least I must have clear proof that the Holy Father knows the truth concerning these matters. I believe that I also have a right to have the Doctrinal Congregation officially inform me that the accusation is unjust in the matter itself and damaging in tone.

It would be extraordinarily painful for me if, in case of a reluctance to provide any redress, I were to feel myself forced to turn to the Church public. Even in this extreme case my purpose could not be other than to serve the Church and to show that one can even today still remain faithful in the Church when one is as unjustly treated as Rosmini and Newman once were. I am prepared to forgive from my heart even before redress is provided. However, this no longer concerns just my own person, but also the

effective functioning of critical offices in the
Church and so that others should be spared similar experiences.

7. I have honestly made the effort to put
myself into the mentality of the author of the indictment. But I have in no way succeeded in understanding how, in view of the many pages already referred to, this accusation could be thus
formulated: "The possibility of a moral theological discourse on the basis of its own autonomy
and authority is thus denied (cf. pp. 5, 6, 15, 18,
22, 160)."

In the introductory pages 5–6, I emphasize
the necessity of an interdisciplinary dialogue in
order to work jointly through new problems.

Pages 15 and 16 are under the heading
"Medicine in Health Criticism and in Interdisciplinary Dialogue." I hope to have made clear
there that in the course of the millennia the medical profession itself had inquired into the morally
good and true. There is no talk whatsoever there
about dialogue with the theological faculty or
with the Magisterium. Here again it becomes
clear that the accuser never paid any attention to
the context.

On page 22 there are clear statements on the
topic, such that the indictment contradicts itself
when it wants to base itself on this page. I request
Your Eminence again to personally read through
these pages, for you yourself have supported the
indictment through your signature. In order to
respond to the accusation concerning page 160 I
would have to know to which edition the Doctrinal Congregation is referring. The fourth edi-

tion was published long before the indictment. Page 160 (4th edition) gives a special reason for interdisciplinary dialogue, namely, the joint concern for the protection of the beginning life in the womb. I do not deny that theology or the Magisterium can, without dialogue with the professional experts, also teach autonomously the immorality of interrupting pregnancy. But theology as a service of healing is not possible if it ignores what the medical and other scientific experts have to say to us about the matter. Page 160 in the earlier editions treats other matters, but nothing said there provides an occasion for accusation.

In general what I have to say about the necessity of dialogue between theologians and the Magisterium with the medical profession is clearly an obvious application of what the Council in *Lumen gentium*, N. 32–37, in *Gaudium et spes*, N. 44, and elsewhere repeatedly said. The accused pages lie in general along the line of the encyclical of Pope Paul VI, *Ecclesiam suam*. The Church cannot carry out its responsibility for healing or its healing service in monologue. It needs a dialogue in which the theologians and officials always have something to learn, which will improve their fulfillment of their healing responsibilities.

8. In an indictment in which the Holy Father is supposed to participate against me the following accusations may not be left out: "What is stated on pp. 149–150, despite the appearance of fidelity, stands against the teaching of *Humanae vitae*." ("*Più che viene detto a p. 149–150, nonos-*

*tante le apperenze di fedeltà, si pone contro l'in-
segnamento del'Enciclica Humanae Vitae.")* I
could easily defend myself with reference to the
precise formulation of my text in *Etica medica*.
Even the manner of expression of the indictment
makes it clear that we are dealing with a case
against my intention and not against my expression. I definitely do not say more than significant
episcopacies have said in their pastoral declarations on *Humanae vitae*. I believe also that the
restrained manner in which I speak in *Etica medica* could contribute to reconciliation within the
Church. On the contrary, a trial against unex-
pressed intentions and an obligation to take on a
narrow-minded interpretation of the encyclical
would mean that a large portion, if not the majority, of theologians and faithful would have to be
brought before the tribunal of the Doctrinal Congregation, which would lead to a destructive loss
of authority, not to speak about the danger of increasing polarization.

For both myself and the Doctrinal Congregation I do not wish to make light of this question
of self-defense: loyalty to the Church is not possible without absolute honesty. And sometimes it
demands candor. In January of 1967—I could be
mistaken about the date—I was summoned by
the then-secretary of the *Suprema Sacra Congregatio Sancti Officii*, Msgr. Parente. I received a
monitum delivered in a most severe tone before I
was heard. It concerned an interview which the
magazine *La Rocca* had published. In substance I
had said: "It would be inopportune to make any
comment now concerning birth control; for the

Pope will speak about this presumably in the near future. But, one thing appeared certain to me, that one must expect that the Pope certainly would not speak in a manner which would run contrary to the statement of the Council." These words are a summary. The accusation which was raised against me was that I wanted to subordinate the Pope to the Council. It was screamed at me: "The Pope is not bound to the Council. You cannot say that the Pope must hold himself to the Council." I am prepared for a personal confrontation with Cardinal Parente and with a statement under oath. At that time I reacted with the remark: "Now I understand more about certain intentions." I could easily fill out the details of that picture.

In order to understand me better I ask that the following fact be noted. Franciscan fathers from Sant'Antonio, where Father Lio, Consultor of the Doctrinal Congregation lived, reported to me long before the publication of the encyclical about a very indiscreet statement by Father Lio. I cite in substance: he spoke to his confreres about how the Pope had almost succumbed to the errors of the Papal Commission on Birth Control; but in a brief time he was able to "reconvert" (*riconvertire*) the Pope.

That is only a part of the background of my reaction to the publication of *Humanae vitae*. About six days before the publication, the complete text of the encyclical was given to me by a large North American weekly magazine with the expectation that I would grant a statement or take a position that would appear almost immediately after the publication of the encyclical. I rejected this expectation, and not solely because I was told that the text was delivered to the magazine by a monsignor of the Vatican for $2,000. I hid myself in an out-of-the-way retreat house in order not to be bothered any further and to devote myself to prayer. I came to the conclusion never to say a word about the encyclical, not even about the background which was known to me. I read the encyclical repeatedly in the hope that I could in the end accept its decisions and argumentation with an honest conscience. It was not possible. Therefore I wished to remain silent. I even remained silent for several days after the publication. However, as a highly placed official in the Church demanded in a severe tone that those persons who did not wish to accept the encyclical in faith should leave the Church, and I also learned that in fact a large number of physicians declared that they were leaving the Church, I changed my mind, again after long prayer. Whatever I said or wrote about the encyclical in the following days I sent ahead of time to the Secretary of State of His Holiness Paul VI.

In the beginning of October, 1968, I had a long and candid discussion with the then Secretary of State Cardinal Cicognani. To my surprise he told me at the outset that the Holy Father was filled with pain about my constant battle against celibacy. I could not believe my ears. I offered to bring to the Cardinal proof, statements of witnesses that there could hardly be another theologian who had spoken and written so much in favor of celibacy and faithfulness to the promises given. I protested against the slander. The Cardinal secretary promised me that he would see to it that the Pope was better informed on this point. He did not wish, however, that I would seek an audience with the Pope. Then we spoke about *Humanae vitae* and about honesty and uprightness in the Church and certain measures—e.g., the case in Washington, DC—which could lead to intimidation and hypocrisy. The Cardinal promised to work for the settlement of the case.

In view of the declarations of many bishops' conferences and on the basis of the clarifying discussion with Cardinal Secretary of State Cicognani and on the basis of discussions with a large number of highly respected ecclesial personalities, I finally felt myself justified in conscience and could *honestly* accept the encyclical as it was accepted by the great episcopacies in their pastoral declarations.

The manner and form in which the indictment treated me negatively in this matter filled me with anxiety, not for myself, but rather for the sake of harmony in the Church and out of concern for good relations between the central administration of the Church and the honest forces in the Church which are more critical in individual questions than are the theologians of the Doctrinal Congregation. If a case is brought against me in this regard, then a great portion of theologians and laity who are loyal to the Church also stand accused. If that occurs, then those who refuse to express their convictions in order not to damage their advancement will be the ones who will make a career for themselves.

9. In order to respond to the last point, I will also take a position on the final accusation: "In substance, there is a refusal to consider the structure of the act as the source of morality." ("*In sostanza, si rifiutato di considerare la struttura dell'atto come fonte di moralità.*") Where and how have I ever hesitated to do this? The true substance is much more that I search for the total structure of the act and not merely a partial aspect of it as the final criterion. The total structure of the act as a human act—not as those acts which "nature teaches all animals"—is decisive. However, I also take the biological structure as well as the psychic structure of the human act very seriously. From that there flows, among other things, my preparedness for an interdisciplinary dialogue. For the medical and other scientific professionals can tell us many very significant things about the biological or psychic structure of a human act.

Your Eminence,

These are my responses. I hope that they are clear and clarifying. Likewise I hope that you understand my feelings. During the Second World War I stood before a military court four times. Twice it was a case of life and death. At that time I felt honored because I was accused by enemies of God. The accusations then were to a very large extent true, because I was not submissive to that regime. Now I am accused by the Doctrinal Congregation in an extremely humiliating manner. The accusations are untrue. In addition, they come from a very high organ of the Church leadership, an organ of that Church which I in a long life have served with all of my power and honesty and hope to serve still further with sacrifice. I would rather stand once again before a court of war of Hitler. But my faith is not shaken.

When at the beginning of the Year of Reconciliation the *Osservatore Romano* attacked me in a lead article in a manner that aroused astonishment I remained silent, although I could have spoken out and although influential elements of the mass media pressed me with their invitations to respond. The commandment for reconciliation is valid today and always, even in the case of the accusation by the Doctrinal Congregation which was sent toward the end of the Year of Reconciliation. If, however, silence will be misunderstood and not serve reconciliation, then speaking becomes gold. I would view servility as betrayal of the Church. Therefore I have answered here clearly and indeed with an inner calm and peace of heart. I must not allow any doubt to arise that this time I will demand that my right to reparations be honored. "Opus justitiae pax" [The work of justice is peace].

I take the opportunity to express to you personally, Your Eminence, my great appreciation. I ask for your blessing and hope that you will be the Daniel who brought forth the oldest to speak.

In the peace of Christ I remain,

Yours sincerely,
Bernhard Häring, C.Ss.R.

On March 5 Cardinal Seper sent me a personal interim response "for my better information and also to calm me," for what was involved here was a doctrinal trial and not a penal trial. He closed with the remark that this case would be carried out in complete secrecy. Therefore no public damage to my reputation would result. My vehement complaint that my honor had been damaged in the eyes of the Pope was not referred to.

I do not wish in any way to denigrate this interim response as far as its good will is concerned. Nevertheless, just as I wished to make available to the Cardinal the following reflection for the sake of a correct history of this style of a doctrinal trial, so also I wish to reproduce it here.

(Document 2)
His Eminence Card. Seper
Congregation for the Doctrine of the Faith
                              March 13, 1976

Your Eminence,
    The doctrinal trial currently going on against me certainly will interest the writers of history, and since it will cast a characterizing light on the present situation in the Church I would like to share my reflections on the "interim information."
    The letter speaks of "calming me" and emphasizes that a doctrinal trial does not aim at upsetting the author. Must it not, however, have an upsetting effect in the extreme if an official doctrinal trial is initiated and the presentation of the accusations is approved by the Pope before the author is heard in any manner? However, one could overlook even this if before the formal introduction of a doctrinal trial the points of accusation had at least been checked out by a theolo-

gian friendly to the author or at minimum by an educated and objective-thinking theologian. As my first response certainly has satisfactorily indicated, the accusations created completely out of thin air in reference to several places in the book would be immediately recognized as untenable by every objective-thinking and educated theologian or even by every religiously and culturally educated layperson.

Must not such an initiation of a doctrinal trial deeply disturb every Christian who loves the Church as an institution?

In addition, in the "information" it is pointed out that this case is not a "penal trial." What is missing in the letter is that tiny word "only." Nevertheless, the calming is supposed to come from the knowledge that it is "only" a doctrinal trial that is in question!

Is it not all the more disturbing when one says to an author known world-wide that a doctrinal trial initiated against him should not disturb him? Is not a completely ungrounded suspicion of the orthodoxy of a Catholic theologian, especially when the accusation is institutionally brought forth in such an astounding manner, just as serious as a superficially initiated penal trial?

A "dialectical stage" is spoken of. The word "dialectic" alienates me here for the doctrinal trial in fact is only one portion of a more than unfriendly attitude toward the author. Is not what is really involved here a battle directed against a very particular theology? This clearly can be seen from the indictment. The unfriendliness and injustice of the accusation remind one

here—please forgive the phrase—of a kind of
Marxist dialectic in which mutual respectful appreciation and the common search for the truth
does not find a home.

Always yours in the Lord,

Sincerely,
Bernhard Häring

On May 1, I myself wrote to the Prefect of the Doctrinal Congregation and sent him my critical essay on the
Vatican document *Persona humana*. I was determined to
show my cards openly. [Editor's Note: Persona humana *is
the Latin name for the Congregation for the Doctrine of the
Faith's "Declaration on Certain Questions Concerning Sexual Ethics," December 29, 1975. Washington: U.S.C.C.
Publication #438-4.*]

(Document 3)
To His Eminence
Cardinal Franjo Seper
Prefect of the Doctrinal Congregation

May 1, 1976

Your Eminence,
The radical openness with which I wish to
respond to the doctrinal trial initiated against me
and still not closed leads me to send to you
the enclosed essay, my reflections on *Persona
humana*.

The indictment sent me and which is the
basis of the doctrinal trial reveals a complete theology. That for me was a reason to pursue the
question whether the doctrinal document on several sexual questions did not show similar or

identical theological tendencies. I originally had the aim in regard to *Persona humana*—despite my unease concerning several formulations—to express only my fundamental confirmation, since I am indeed in agreement with the central aim. I rejected all further pressure from press agencies and journalists. The reason was not cowardice, but rather pastoral concern regarding the extremely negative reactions of the press in various countries. My brief, positive stance, which made the rounds in the press, stirred wide astonishment and incredulity. They did not wish to believe that all of a sudden I could be so uncritical and submissive. If it would serve truth and healing (including credibility) I could allow such reactions simply to remain. However, because of the astounding reasons given for the doctrinal trial against me, and still more out of concern for healing, and for credibility, I found myself ultimately motivated to accept the repeated requests of different editors to publish a scholarly position in regard to *Persona humana*. Since these reflections of mine expand my answer to your indictment, I would like to bring them to your attention.

With the expression of my respect for your person and for your office, I am in the Lord,

Yours sincerely,
Bernhard Häring, C.Ss.R.

("Reflexionen zur Erklärung der Glaubenskongregation über einige Fragen der Sexualethik," *Theologisch-praktische Quartalschrift*, 1976, pp. 115–126.)

My article in the *Theologisch-praktische Quartal-schrift* brought me many letters of thanks from pastors and theologians. I would like to cite one sentence from a letter of the highly respected Professor Richard Egenter, who is very pastorally oriented: "It was with intense agreement that I read your article on the Roman paper on sexuality in the *Theologisch-praktische Quartalschrift*. I thank you from the heart and with full appreciation for your having written with this consciously responsible candor. . . . The effect of *Persona humana* here in the Federal Republic of Germany has been devastating in a double sense. The public in general, including serious Catholics, has only contempt for it, while at the same time it welds together the rigid conservatives and places a weapon in their hands."

Another, a moral theologian who is still living, wrote me among other things: "Among the many critical responses, I hold yours to have provided the greatest service in the tension between scholarship-Magisterium-grassroots. Both in content and style, your clarity is linked together with your option for the institutional Church."

The Doctrinal Congregation thought otherwise. Even on the occasion of my last conversation in my doctrinal trial its displeasure showed itself very clearly.

However, soon another occasion led to a further magnification of the tension: I was at that time a regular collaborator of the largest Catholic weekly *Famiglia Cristiana*. Every week I wrote a response to one or more letters concerning questions on the formation of a Christian life. According to the analysis of an institute for opinion research, I had between seven and nine million readers. On May 23, I responded to a whole series of letters from married couples who wrote that the literal observations of the norms of *Humanae vitae* against contraception had alienated their marriage partner, turned him into an enemy of the Church, and threatened to destroy the marriage. I answered very briefly in that I quoted a more lengthy sentence from the position taken by the French episcopacy. Since many other bishops' conferences, as well as the Joint Synod of the West German Dioceses, had issued similar sounding statements, I did not expect any increase of the tension between the Doctrinal Congregation and myself through this citation. However, I had deceived myself, as the two following communications from Cardinal Seper of July 3, and November 11, 1976 show.

The first document has a special historical significance. First, it was composed in French, which probably should lead one to conclude that it was really the French bishops and all those who would like to depend on them that are singled out and warned here.

Second, it is a very clear expression of the firm determination of the Doctrinal Congregation, in regard to the prohibition of artificial contraception, to stand rigidly with absolute inflexibility and absolute exclusion of every kind of application of *epikeia* or *oikonomia*. No one should be allowed to think that an infringement of the objective scale of values would be permitted. At most, what might be granted is the possibility of a lessened subjective guilt.

It should also be noted that on July 14, 1976, the *Osservatore Romano* published an extremely polemical article by the Milanese moralist G. B. Guzzetti against me in precisely this sense ("New Attacks on *Humanae vitae,*" *Osservatore Romano*, July 14, p. 2). It is worth noting, however, that in this article there was no mention whatsoever that my response was an exact quotation of the official declaration of the French episcopacy, whereas the Doctrinal Congregation noted that fact. In this regard the

cards were now on the table. Calling upon the statements
of a large episcopacy would be looked upon as a punishable act—here is the text.

(Document 4)
Sacred Congregation for the
    Doctrine of the Faith
Prot. N. 13/59

July 3, 1976

Reverend Father,
    In your response to a reader of the magazine
Famiglia Cristiana of May 23 (p. 9) you speak of
the "traditional teaching" to which the French
bishops refer, according to which "in cases of
conflict of duties the more weighty and pressing
duty has priority. Thus it could happen that
spouses with a good conscience and without guilt
would choose the most appropriate means for
birth control."
    Paragraph 16 of the "Pastoral Note of the
French Episcopacy on *Humanae vitae*" (November, 1968), doubtlessly lacks precision in regard to the objective and subjective aspect of a
conflict of conscience. Nevertheless, I deem it
important that you refer to the precision of the
authorized text, which the French Bishops' conference through Cardinal Renard, who was then
chair of the Commission for the Family, had issued. Perhaps this text escaped your attention
(*Documentation Catholique*, 1968, col. 2174). In
addition to this (cf. ibid., col. 2174) it even said
very clearly in regard to section 16 of the "note":
"Whatever the case may be with *subjective*

guilt, a contraceptive pact can never be *objectively* good."

The Doctrinal Congregation takes the position that the declaration of the French bishops may not be used without this improvement. We also view it as necessary to demand from you a correction of your response in *Famiglia Cristiana*, and all the more so because this statement drew the attention of the press agency ANSA and as a consequence of a number of newspapers.

In regard to the communication to my Superior General, through whom the above text was passed on to me, I refer to the complete documentation in the Italian edition of this book, *Fede Storia Morale*. Here then is my response of September 14, 1976.

(Document 5)
To His Eminence Cardinal Franjo Seper
Prefect of the Doctrinal Congregation
Rome, September 14, 1976
Feast of the Finding
of the Holy Cross

Your Eminence,
Your communication of July 3, 1976, reached me only in the middle of August in an outlying mission station of Asia. I had no opportunity there to look for the text you referred to. Immediately upon my return here I did so.

I knew the statement by Cardinal Renard from *Documentation Catholique* and from a little book with the title: Karl Rahner-Cardinal Renard-Bernhard Häring, *A propos de l'encycli-*

que Humanae vitae (Paris: Apostolat des Editions, 1969). I did not know the published rectification of the statement in *Documentation Catholique* (1968, col. 2174). The text published in the above mentioned book has a third reading, which appears a happier one to me. Basically, however, the Cardinal says the same thing, with the declaration: "The bishops have traced in par. 16, a process, if one can say this, from a subjective state lived by the spouses, to an objective state, so to speak, corresponding to the will of God." (*"Les évêques ont tracé dans le paragraphe 16, un cheminement si l'on peut ainsi dire, d'un état subjectif vécu par les époux, à un état objectif c'est-à-dire correspondant à la volonté de Dieu."*—l.c.p. 64) To my knowledge the lecture given by the Chair of the French Bishops' Conference does not belong to the bishops' declaration as an integrated part. And the fact that there are three different readings shows his own struggle for an understanding.

If we allow the declaration of the French episcopacy to be interpreted as Cardinal Renard does it, then that is also valid for my response in *Famiglia Cristiana*; for I respond not in the abstract, but rather corresponding to the "subjective state lived by the spouses." (" . . . *état subjectif vécu par les époux.*") If one views objective "objectif" as "meta ideale," as do the Italian bishops in their declaration, it then adds an additional meaning. I fear, however, that this tearing apart of "subjective" and "objective" cannot be easily read into the declaration of the French bishops. It also opens all gates and doors to "subjectivism."

It is better to leave the text of the French bishops in the tradition of intending the correct resolution of a case of the conflict of duties.

What should I respond to the many inquiries concerning the following cases: a married woman who believes she must absolutely exclude the possibility of conception demands abstinence from her husband. She alienates him thereby from herself and from the Church. Must she simply accept that "objectively"? Or does she behave correctly if she now attempts to win back her husband to the marriage and to the Church in that she agrees with him temporarily to use a non-abortive means of birth control? If I first say: "Objectively that is absolutely to be avoided," then I can no longer sensibly offer the direction of the French bishops.

It is in the knowledge of and with attention to the declaration of Cardinal Renard (first and third versions) that I have in my response in *Famiglia Cristiana*, June 20, 1976, pp. 5–6, lifted out precisely that sentence of the Declaration of the French bishops to which Cardinal Renard later referred. I wrote: "I do not say that contraception is a good; I only say that in the case of the conflicts described to me that the married people can act with a good conscience and without guilt." Then I added the citation: "Contraception can never be a good. It is always a disorder; but this disorder is not always guilt-laden. . . . "

This carefully weighed response of mine, which is completely respectful toward the authority of the Pope, earned a reaction in the *Osserva-*

tore Romano which was not only unscholarly in tone, but also incomprehensible (July 14, 1976, p. 2). The article is by Msgr. G. M. Guzzetti. At the same time his friends published similar articles in other press vehicles. What is astounding in this is that there is no mention that the article of June 20 was essentially nothing other than a quotation of the Declaration of the French bishops. Was the aim to reject the opinion of the French bishops, or to smear an individual theologian?

Your communication of July 3 is composed such that one must suppose that my article of June 20 was not yet known. In view of this fact and especially in view of the campaign directed by Msgr. Guzzetti and his friends, I presume that the Doctrinal Congregation no longer insists that I should once again return to this matter in *Famiglia Cristiana*. I could not in conscience go further than in my article of June 20. For the sake of peace I am prepared to let the matter rest. History can one day judge more calmly. I know in conscience that everyone must answer before the judgment of God. If a doctrinal trial continues against me in this matter, then the majority of the theological community would have to be drawn into the doctrinal trial with me.

If the Doctrinal Congregation nevertheless insists upon a rectification, then I, in all honesty, would have to lay out my convictions of conscience, namely, that in cases of the conflict of duties objective criteria are available. Further, I would have to respond to the polemic instigated against me by Guzzetti and his group. Nevertheless, I am prepared to publish a "rectification" composed by and authorized by the Doctrinal Congregation in *Famiglia Cristiana* and (or) other press outlets, with, however, the clear indication that this is an act of external obedience and not a change of my personal convictions, if the rectification insisted upon contradicts my conviction. Whatever does not come from honest conviction is a sin.

Always in the Lord,

Yours sincerely,
Bernhard Häring, C.Ss.R.

A communication from the Doctrinal Congregation on the same matter was much more severe when the *Neue Illustrierte* took over my statement from the *Famiglia Cristiana*, and did so in the form of an interview which had never taken place.

(Document 6)
Sacred Congregation for the
   Doctrine of the Faith
Prot. N. 13/59
                                        November 11, 1976

Reverend Father,
   On September 14 you responded to the letter of this Dikasterium concerning your treatment in *Famiglia Cristiana* of the question of the use of contraception in cases where there is a conflict of obligations.
   I do not wish to place in doubt your good faith. But since you remain firm in your ideas, I feel obliged to make clear to you that the Doctrinal Congregation cannot approve your manner

of handling this problematic and it especially objects to your presenting your opinion as Catholic thinking in such a widely read magazine as *Famiglia Cristiana*. And, as if that were not enough, you have repeated your ideas in an interview given to the *Neue Illustrierte Revue* (June 21, 1976), which moreover is a pornographic organ of the press.

I am informing you that I have demanded of your Superior General that he call you to order for the sake of a greater wisdom. At the same time, in carrying out my responsibilities I wish to make clear to you that it is inappropriate for you to publish in such a publication or in the general press in order to promote your ideas.

My Superior General carried out this charge in the most polite manner possible. I explained in my first response that I had never given such an interview. Cardinal Seper thanked me for this information on February 8, 1977. Then when I received a formal declaration from the editor of the *Neue Illustrierte Revue* that in fact no interview had taken place and I sent this document on to the Doctrinal Congregation, Cardinal Seper wrote to me: "I want to warmly thank you for this information and remain with best wishes." More cannot really be expected from the Vatican. A formal apology has no place in the curial tradition and even with such a polite man as Cardinal Seper it was absent.

However, back to the main trial in regard to my book *Etica Medica*. I received as an answer to my detailed response of February 5, 1976, a still longer "register of sins" on May 18, 1977—fifteen months later. The mills of Rome grind slowly. I am providing here the main text and refer to the long, turgid "annex" in the Italian edition of this book (*Fede Storia Morale*, Rome: Borla, 1989, pp. 255–259). According to Cardinal Hamer it was written up by "two great moralists"—the sort who confuse *Zeitgeist* with *Zeichen der Zeit* ("the signs of the time"). Their way of thinking is purely deductive, abstract, out of touch with life, statistical, and ahistorical.

(Document 7)
Sacred Congregation for the
    Doctrine of the Faith
Prot. N. 13/59

May 18, 1977

Most Reverend Father,
    With its communication of December 16, 1975, in regard to your book *Etica Medica*, this Congregation required of you several fundamental clarifications and decisions concerning the discourse of moral theology, as well as questions of medical deontology which come up in the book. Your response of February 5, 1976, provided a number of specifications on some points, but the result was not satisfactory. Hence, we planned to invite you to a conversation at this Congregation in order to clarify the unresolved problems, eliminate all ambiguities and above all initiate with you an open, positive dialogue in the service of the unity in faith. Unfortunately we learned of your departure too late, and thus it was necessary, in order not to draw out the matter too much, to choose the written path. We hope that this will attain the same goal.
    As you know, the responsibility of this Con-

gregation consists in the promotion and protection of faith and morals (*costumi*) in the Catholic world (cf. *Integrae servandae, AAS*, 57 [1965], p. 952 and *Regimini Ecclesiae Universae, AAS*, 59 [1967], pp. 885-952), and in this especially to look after those who by themselves do not have a sufficient capacity or theological preparation to be able to distinguish in the various publications between what belongs to the indispensable patrimony of the faith and what is only a theological opinion worthy of more or less consideration. The intervention of this Congregation in your case is inspired by this precise concern.

You know indeed how important it is for the proclamation of salvation to our contemporaries that a constructive relationship between the Magisterium and theologians in their different competencies and in a climate of responsible collaboration be firmly established. The Holy Father has already recalled this in his address to the International Congress on the Theology of the Second Vatican Council (*AAS*, 58 [1966], p. 890). Certainly the work of the International Theological Commission in Rome (cf. *Gregorianum*, 57 [1976], pp. 549–563) is known to you in which twelve theses were put forward that illuminate the relationship between the mission given to the ecclesial Magisterium for the protection of Divine Revelation and the task assigned to theologians who are to study and explain the doctrines of faith. The Magisterium as well as the theologians must constantly hold to these different functions and the common responsibility toward the *word of God*, the *sensus fidelium* of the Christian people, the documents of *Tradition*, as well as the *pastoral and missionary tasks*.

Perhaps it would not be without usefulness to repeat here verbatim the text in regard to the respective functions of the Magisterium and theologians:

"1. It is the Magisterium's task authoritatively to defend the catholic integrity and unity of faith and morals. From this follow specific functions; and, although at first glance they seem particularly to be of a rather negative character, they are, rather, a positive ministry for the life of the Church. These are: 'the task of authoritatively interpreting the word of God, written and handed down' (DV,10), the censuring of opinions which endanger the faith and morals proper to the Church, and the proposing of truths which are of particular contemporary relevance. Although it is not the work of the Magisterium to propose theological syntheses, still, because of its concern for unity, it must consider individual truths in the light of the whole, since integrating a particular truth into the whole belongs to the very nature of truth.

2. The theologians' function in some way mediates between the Magisterium and the people of God. For 'theology has a two-fold relation with the Magisterium of the Church and with the universal community of Christians. In the first place, it occupies a sort of midway position between the faith of the Church and its Magisterium.' (Paul VI, l.c. 892). . . .

On the other hand, by their work of interpretation, teaching and translation into contemporary modes of thought, theologians insert the teaching and warnings of the Magisterium into a wider, synthetic context and thus contribute to a better knowledge on the part of the people of God. In this way, 'they lend their aid to the task of spreading, clarifying, confirming and defending the truth which the Magisterium authoritatively propounds' (Paul VI, l.c. 89I)."

[From Thesis 5 of *Theses on the Relationship Between the Ecclesiastical Magisterium and Theology*, Washington: USCC, 1977).]

Most Reverend Father, the Holy Doctrinal Office gladly acknowledges that a good portion of your activity lies along this line—like your contribution to ethical-theological reflections, and your attentiveness and alert pastoral sense for the always new problems of the contemporary world.

Nevertheless, this Congregation cannot hide the fact that various pages of your book *Etica Medica* caused us perplexity, despite the improvements in the last edition (4th edition, Rome, 1975).

In the appendix or addendum you will find a number of remarks in this connection. However, what is now closest to the heart of this Congregation is not so much to discuss anew the questions raised in this connection by your book, but rather much more to recall to your consciousness your task as a theologian and therefore as a witness to the faith in everything which you write and teach, and how your task is to be seen within the context of a double relationship—to the Magisterium and to the Christian community. To the Magisterium: not to place oneself outside of or in contrast to what the universal Church authoritatively teaches and proclaims. To the Christian community: through constant care—and most especially when you write for magazines with a broader distribution—for how the general public (above all when it is not familiar with the theological problematic, which in general is the case with those whom you address) could take up that which you say and could thus arrive at convictions and ethical decisions which do not correspond to the fundamental, indispensable principles of Catholic moral teaching.

Therefore, the Doctrinal Congregation requires of you above all a greater attention and prudence. You must make every effort to avoid spreading questionable and subjective opinions, especially in such widely read magazines as *Famiglia Cristiana*, in other popular publications, or in public appearances. This Congregation requires that you declare your adherence to Catholic doctrine in regard to the points in question as the Magisterium has authentically expressed them and that in the future you avoid every oral or written statement which could raise a doubt about this adherence.

An expression of your acceptance of these points and of your willingness to clarify and set aright your opinions on the issues in question, for the sake of the faithful, would enable us to re-

quest from a higher authority the close of this
procedure.

Such an expression could be made, for example, on the occasion of new publications or by
making the necessary improvements in a future
new edition of the book. Thus this congregation
awaits a written assurance of your acceptance of
the matters here discussed.

Sincerely,
F. Cardinal Seper, Prefect

Of course, there is much to say about all this. According to the appended material, I would have to restrict my
entire moral theological work to an extremely narrow concept of salvation. I would have to return to a static concept
of the natural moral law, and not only avoid all dissent, but
also everything which could even have the appearance of
a dissent. Indeed, the prospect of my even surviving the
doctrinal trial was poor—since at this precise moment the
first signs of throat cancer became discernible.

I sent the following declaration to the Doctrinal Congregation on June 2, 1977:

(Document 8)
I received your communication of May 18,
1977, with the protocol #13/59. I hereby make
the following declaration:

I have never doubted the dogmas of the
Church as they have been presented by the
Magisterium, nor have I expressed doubt.

I will always show attentiveness and respect
in the highest degree to teachings which are presented without the qualification "infallible." Re-

formable teachings, however, cannot demand an act of faith nor absolute agreement. All the world knows that in the past the Magisterium itself has reformed several doctrines which it had previously presented in emphatic fashion; and that was made possible by the strength of the loyalty and honesty of many theologians.

I will always attempt to honor the Church, the People of God, and its Magisterium through absolute honesty, even if that should bring me a threat. This loyalty and honesty is for me a holy duty, even in all those questions in which, after serious reflection and prayer, I have come to the conviction that I cannot accept the all too narrow interpretations of the Doctrinal Congregation. This is especially so when I know myself to be at one with many bishops, with the majority of theologians, and with a large number of laity zealous for the faith. I would not have such great trust in my own insights if I found myself in contradiction to the great majority of theologians or to the *sensus fidelium* of the Christian people.

Thus I cannot, for example, see that it is the task of the Magisterium "authoritatively to defend the unity of morals," as your letter appears to maintain. The unity in belief is one thing, but the unity of morals beyond the generally acknowledged fundamental principles in the great tradition is another.

I do not deny, but confirm and confess the jurisdiction of the Magisterium in questions which concern the law of God resting in the hearts of human beings. In fact I see the Magisterium as an inalienable and necessary part of the

Pilgrim People of God who should progress in the knowledge of God and human nature. This progress can demand new clarifications and distinctions.

The natural law is a part of the law of Christ. This does not exclude, however, that new historical factors, a better understanding of the human, and the various traditions, must be taken into account. The law written in the hearts of human beings is not a codex of formulations, but rather can and must be laid out and formulated in living languages.

I do not have the Italian text of *Etica Medica* at hand. However, if Your Eminence wishes, after my return to Rome on September 7th, I will provide a detailed response to each point.

Of course I will take seriously your admonition to be careful in my expression. At the same time I will also commit myself to honesty in order to serve the cause of the Church and the faithful.

In a communication of July 5, 1977, Cardinal Seper pressed for the earliest possible response to all the questions raised. In a response of July 25, I requested more time for reflection, for consultation with devout and wise persons, and also in order to provide a careful formulation in the light of the law of the Church so that—even if it is after my death—the trial can be correctly judged.

At the time, due to throat cancer, I was practically speechless. Still, I wanted to provide a comprehensive response before the beginning of the required surgery, in the hope that I could finally get the matter behind me.

Here is my correspondence with the Doctrinal Congregation of August, 1977, to August, 1978.

(Document 9)
To His Eminence Cardinal F. Seper
Prefect of the Doctrinal Congregation
Edmonton, August 20, 1977

Your Eminence,
Here is my response to the specific points in your communication of May 22, 1977, as you required in your communication of July 5, 1977.

In the first place, I thank God that during the two years of the doctrinal trial by the Doctrinal Congregation God has granted me in rich measure the experience of an inner peace and of freedom. I thank God too for the suffering and the love of the Church which this doctrinal trial has brought me. This experience will certainly have a very strong influence on the further service which I will offer to the Church. It likewise builds on the experience I had with the Holy Office and especially with several of its representatives, from 1959 to the end of the Council. It has transformed my love for the Church into a suffering and critical love.

As already mentioned, I cannot but bring this doctrinal trial into connection with all the experiences of hostility and misunderstanding, with the obvious and planned slandering, with several astonishing articles in the *Osservatore Romano*, and the like, all of which were supposed to undermine my influence. Early on I learned from the sociology of knowledge how to distinguish knowledge of salvation, abstract knowledge of existence, and the knowledge of domination. I will turn myself anew to this problem in the light of

my experiences and in the hope of performing a
genuine service for the Church as well as for the
Doctrinal Congregation.

The following reflections are not primarily
my self-defense, but rather an attempt at a candid
dialogue in the service of the Church. After a
long period of reflection and prayer, and following the advice of the most saintly people whom I
know, I hope that these reflections will be given
serious consideration. That is, I hope that Your
Eminence, my accuser and judge, would read this
appeal not as a judge and accuser but, rather, as a
fellow Christian and responsible servant of the
Church.

I. The first reflection concerns my repeated
shock because of the tension between a formal or
official competence and a substantive competence. I am speechless in the face of the fact that
the Doctrinal Congregation in a matter against a
well-known theologian can depend upon an expert advisor or official accuser who is not even
able to distinguish between *Zeitgeist* and "the
signs of the time" (*Zeichen der Zeit*). Further, I
point to the astounding accusations, according to
which the stress on an interdisciplinary dialogue
would deny the autonomy of moral theology.
That implies that this advisor to the Doctrinal
Congregation views expert knowledge in medicine as unnecessary when dealing with new problems of medical ethics.

The most weighty aspect, however, is the
defective distinction between mores (*costumi*,
customs) on the one hand and morality on the

other. I will return to this question in view of its wide-ranging consequences when I respond to the details of your communication and the appendix of May 22.

From the entire correspondence it appears clear that these experts are not conscious that their manner of thinking and arguing presents an entirely limited mode of thought. This is certainly not representative today. There must be space granted in the Church for other models of thinking if the Church wishes to exercise a positive influence in the dialogue with the modern world.

II. A second series of reflections concerns the human and Christian aspects of the doctrinal trial. I do not wish here to go into the particular background of the doctrinal trial, that is, the indiscretion which I brought to your attention very early. I limit myself here only to your own documentation.

1. In my judgment the tone of the accusing document and also of the last annex violate the humane norms of politeness, and even more the proper concern for truth when such a serious accusation and trial is concerned. The apostle admonishes, "You fathers, do not irritate your children!" I cannot see how such a tone and such a trial go together with the daily prayer, "and lead us not into temptation."

2. After that, sanctions were imposed without hearing the accused and without naming a defender. I refer to the alleged interview with the magazine *Neue Revue*. To bring my Superior

General into the matter and demand of him that he bring me to heel was a very severe sanction. This took place before I had any chance to respond in the matter. Still more weighty is the fact that after clear proof was submitted that I had not given the alleged interview, no apology followed. On the contrary, my Superior General was once again brought into the matter and given new tasks.

If the Doctrinal Congregation can never admit an error and ask for forgiveness, is it any wonder that there is a crisis in the sacramental confession of our sins?

3. Almost at the same time that the *Osservatore* published an article ("New Attacks on the Encyclical *Humanae vitae*") against me, which suppressed the fact that everything in question was a quotation from the French bishops, the Doctrinal Congregation used the same case as an occasion for a severe disciplining and brought my Superior General into the matter. My response, which detailed how I had held myself within the framework and text of the joint statement of the French bishops, was not deemed worthy of a single word of response. Concerning the substance of the matter I would like to pose the following question: Are truth and pastoral sensitivity served if a moderate voice is silenced? The Doctrinal Congregation surely knows well that the general trend is much more negative. If by the desire of the Doctrinal Congregation I were condemned to silence, the radical voices would sound only the louder.

III. Responses to the several important points of your communication of May 18, 1977, Prot. 13/59:

1. Concerning the distinction between theological opinions and "patrimonio inalienabile della fede cattolica" [inalienable patrimony of the Catholic faith]: The question, which is at the heart of the accusation and the severe sanction (bringing in the question of obedience to the Superior General), concerns a citation of the French episcopacy. I could also have cited the West German or Scandinavian or other episcopacies, or could have referred to the West German Joint Synod. It was clear from the context that I was basing myself on *one* explanation among others. It was clear enough that it did not deal with a statement of faith. The faithful certainly know already, or at least have a right to know, that in questions of interpretation there is a pluralism in the Church, which by no means needs to lead to chaos or laxism. My question to the Doctrinal Congregation is precisely in reference to this point. Must it not lead to a much greater confusion among critical and uncritical faithful if the Doctrinal Congregation takes a position on a very concrete question and authoritatively presents a very specific solution while, at the same time, many learned theologians and physicians, on the basis of their expert knowledge, experience, long term reflection and discussion, are of another opinion? I refer, for example, to the declaration about sterilization in Catholic hospitals (Prot. 2027/69) of March 13, 1975. I have seen the

confusion, the anger, the contempt and the sarcasm of physicians of various confessions as well as basic doubts of faith by Catholic physicians. All ask themselves: how does the Doctrinal Congregation have expert knowledge in these matters? What kind of a concept of therapy does the Doctrinal Congregation have when they instruct physicians that the integrity of the *vas deferens* is more important for health and moral integrity than saving someone from mental disease?

My question should be understood generally concerning the many official positions taken earlier by the Inquisition and the Suprema S. Congreg. S. Officii, and recently by the Doctrinal Congregation, on so many questions of biblical interpretation and morality. My many-faceted apostolate has afforded me an insight into the temptations against faith and the Church which flow from all too many of these positions, and from the fact that these bureaus never admit an error, and never acknowledge a declaration as false or precipitous.

Your admonition of theologians to distinguish between the inalienable elements of the faith and theological speculation is correct in theory, but it should also be visibly correct in practice. This is especially a problem because the Consultors of the Holy Office usually have lived their whole lives there, and still do, and do not represent the breadth of Catholic thought. Thus, not infrequently, a very specific theology is made into a standard. The doctrinal trial against me is a clear manifestation of this.

2. Page 2/Paragraph 3: It concerns "the

unity of the faith and of customs" ("unità della fede e dei costumi"). It causes me no difficulty when the "integrità cattolica dei costumi" is spoken of. However, when the document speaks of "l'unità dei costumi," then I am struck with great fear and see many dangers forthcoming, which in fact have already come and were visible in the past. It was a charism of the apostle to the Gentiles that in apostolic times he fended off that danger when the Judaizers wished to force upon all the unity of *costumi* (mores). The Catholic Church dangerously narrowed its mission to proclaim the Gospel to all nations and to make all peoples disciples of Christ when it wished to force upon the Chinese not only the Latin language but also Western rites and *costumi* as a condition for Catholicity. All ethicists and respected Christian moral theologians are agreed that mores may not be equated with morality. Customs stand in an interaction with the total culture. And every external insistence upon a unity of *costumi*, customs or mores, without concern for legitimate cultural pluralism is a response of cultural colonialism and an enormous danger to the evangelization of all peoples and cultures. If the Doctrinal Congregation believes it must guarantee the *"unità dei costumi,"* tendencies will constantly arise to explain customs as fundamental and irrenounceable principles of moral doctrine (*"principi fondamentali e irrinunciabili della dottrina morale"*). What is really a very limited "custom," *un costume*, which perhaps was good and even very good for a particular time and culture, may not correspond to new knowledge, new needs of other places, times and cultures. This tendency can lead to an intensification and re-intensification of earlier declarations of Roman bureaus which simply are not consistent with the development of moral knowledge. I name here, for example, the reference to proposition 40 of the Roman bureaus under Alexander VII: Concerning the grave sinfulness of a kiss when sensual pleasure is thereby experienced (cf. the Declaration on several questions of sexual ethics of December 29, 1975, footnote 19).

3. To the last paragraph of your communication (page 3/4): You require of me a declaration of adherence to Catholic doctrine in the matters referred to as they are authentically declared by the Magisterium (*"adesione alle dottrina cattolica ai ponti in questione sui quali il magistero si è autenticamente pronunciato . . . "*). This demand presumes that in these points I have been guilty of a violation, which could not be proved throughout the entire doctrinal trial. The accusations stand there unproved. They are obviously unjust.

I ask you: If in the future I comment on questions in the document of the West German synod in which the synod takes a more open approach than that of the Holy Office or the Doctrinal Congregation, will that be ground enough to initiate a new doctrinal trial against me? How do you specify the points on which the Magisterium has authentically expressed itself, when inside of the Catholic Church there exist broad differences of interpretation?

Is there never a case in the Catholic Church wherein theologians can express a prophetic dissent? Was Friedrich Spee in his "Cautio Criminalis" a disloyal son of the Church because he expressed his dissent from the then-official teaching about the goodness of torture? As I wrote earlier (in my response of June 2, 1977), I am never inclined to deviate from official teaching, even if this is not infallibly presented, if a large portion of theologians, bishops of sanctity and intelligence, zealous Catholics and whole portions of Christendom have not arrived at other interpretations.

If I have understood correctly, the Doctrinal Congregation teaches that contraception is not only intrinsically and absolutely sinful when conception would be a good thing, but also even in cases in which a conception would without question be immoral. Is there, therefore, according to the official interpretation of the Doctrinal Congregation, absolutely no thinkable case for the application of *epikeia* or *oikonomia*, even when it would save the mental health of one spouse or the marriage itself? Have I understood correctly? In a private letter from Patriarch Athenagoras (of blessed memory) to a friend, which was read to me at his request, the Patriarch expressed his and his Church's conviction that although contraception is morally impermissible, nevertheless, every priest knows that there are cases of *oikonomia* in which the action is free from sin. Precisely that is my interpretation and, if I do not deceive myself, the interpretation of the moderate majority of priests, theologians, and Catholic laity. Should I now declare that I will allow no doubt to arise about my agreement with the interpretation of the Doctrinal Congregation? Were I to promise that, I would in my own eyes be a Judas, a traitor of a carefully formed conscience and disloyal to the Church, which above all needs honest service. If you wish to demand such an adherence from me, then you would have to proceed against the majority of the priests and theologians of a moderate direction.

IV. My reflections on several questions of the "allegato":

1. To the question of the interruption of pregnancy: I do not believe that the expert has correctly summarized my position. The will to accuse is obviously stronger than the ability to understand my manner of thinking. It appears that in this question he possesses no special expert knowledge either in regard to the historical breadth of the doctrine in question or several important facts of biology. I am, nevertheless, quite prepared to meet with him or other persons of the Doctrinal Congregation in a discussion not only to explain my positions, but also to listen and to understand what the precise position of the Doctrinal Congregation is. I am also prepared in future publications to present precisely what the Doctrinal Congregation holds to be true. I would, however, never teach something in my own name which in conscience I did not hold acceptable. For what does not come from an honest conviction is a sin.

The main argument concerns the famous question of "direct abortion." I reject direct abortion. However, as the moral theologians of the Doctrinal Congregation well know, there are two different schools in theology concerning the understanding of "direct" abortion. The one school, to which doubtless the expert (accuser) of my doctrinal trial belongs, gives its definition in view of the material aspect. Thus, one comes to a solution concerning ectopic pregnancy: wait until a tumor has formed around the embryo; then the fallopian tubes, which have become pathological from the tumor, or the ovaries and/or the cervix can be removed by surgery so that an "indirect" abortion is accomplished. I have inquired of many gynecologists of various confessions and different universities. All shook their heads over this manner of thinking.

For me a direct abortion occurs when the *finis operis*, the intended goal of the intervention, is abortion. And with the tradition I hold that such an intervention is immoral. If, however, the *finis operis* of the intervention (and also the *finis operantis*) is life-saving, the intervention can accordingly be undertaken responsibly. I would hold myself in conscience as sharing in the guilt for the death of the mother, were I to accept the physicalist definition of the *actus directus*, and thus maintain that it would be better to allow two human lives to be lost than to rescue at least one. The experience arising from the practice of gynecologists is that especially with an ectopic pregnancy the fetus has absolutely no prospect of survival, while the life of the mother can be saved—and according to the interpretation of all my medical informants—must be saved.

2. Concerning the interpretation of *Humanae vitae*: To a) p.2: My interpretation is identical with the declaration of the German bishops on *Humanae vitae*. It concerns fundamental reflections on the correct understanding of therapy: whether it is a matter of a therapy of organs or, rather, a therapy in view of the total health of the person. A Christian anthropology, in my opinion, goes beyond the biochemical view of the last century. I refer to great Christian and Jewish therapists: Abraham Maslow, Viktor Frankl, Viktor von Weizsäcker, Paul Tournier. Many others could be cited. Again, what is involved here is a conflict between a purely physicalist view of the "directum" and on the other side a determination within the total intention.

To b) p.4 of the "Allegato": here a scientific question of fact is involved, very similar to the question in the Galileo trial. The Magisterium must have the courage here to study the question in an objective and scholarly manner. Concerning this there are many publications. If the Doctrinal Congregation would wish it, I could send in a bibliography.

3. Response to questions of fundamental moral theology: Here I find that the writer for the Doctrinal Congregation is simply out to accuse and, you must excuse the remark, to insult and irritate. The questions which are posed for page 174 could not possibly be addressed to me in this manner if the expert had taken the pains to study

my well-known publications on the natural moral law. The questions themselves would have been impossible if the expert at least had read my book *Etica Medica* with the intention of understanding it. For example, the question, "Does the natural moral law not belong to the law of Christ?" My counter question is: "Has it really escaped the accuser how much I have invested in emphasizing the unity of one moral order, that is, the integration of the natural moral law within the law of Christ?"

To the question: "Can statements of the Magisterium depend on scientific research and scientific statements? I ask: "What about the degree of certitude?" I give the answer precisely as St. Thomas gave it: The more concrete and complex moral problems become, the less is the degree of certitude. I do not deny the competence of the Magisterium in questions of the natural moral law. However, where complex questions of a very concrete nature are involved, substantive knowledge of the matter is needed. That was also stressed by the Council.

To pages 76–81: There is no doubt that contemporary moral theology has attained a more dynamic view of history. Cf. *Gaudium et spes*, art. 4–5. I am accused of teaching that natural law "is only a vague impulse through the evolution of nature and history." Here the possibility of dialogue ceases; for such accusations are unthinkable if one is open to respectful dialogue.

To page 44, par. 5: When one knows the legalism of a portion of moral theology, this pathetic complaint is strange. Many Council Fathers complained about the danger of so-called "rabbinism."

To pages 24–25: "He cites *Gaudium et spes* 26, but does not include the citation about the dependence of things on God. Thus one can do with the Council text what one wishes. . . ." Here my patience ceases. The dependence of all earthly reality on God is not the point in question in my discussion. I cite the Council text insofar as it refers to the question at hand. This is a general custom even in the official documents of the Holy See. Whoever knows my activities even to a limited extent—and an official accuser should take the pain to know them—would find it impossible to make such a statement without an evil intent. Here we are no longer dealing with the knowledge of salvation and healthy relations in the Church. Here bridges are broken down and the moral authority of an important bureau is undermined in order to irritate a disliked author. I forgive. And in this case I do not expect an apology, but I do expect a change in attitude. For this concerns not only me, but the honor of the Holy See, the credibility and the foundational questions of Christian morality: justice and love.

I send this response on the feast day of my patron saint, Saint Bernhard, and ask for his intervention that this my candid statement may be for the welfare of the Church, even if it should bring me further suffering.

With sincere wishes in the Lord,

Bernhard Häring, C.Ss.R.

(Document 10)
Sacred Congregation for the
  Doctrine of the Faith
Prot. N. 13/59

Rome, April 26, 1978

Most Reverend Father Häring,
      Your letter of August 20, 1977, in which you
make a detailed response to the communication
from this Congregation of May 18, 1977, has
gone unanswered until now in view of your illness. Now that you have recovered, I would like
first of all to express to you my sincere joy over
your improved health and best wishes for fruitful
work in the service of Christ and his Church.
      The Congregation for the Doctrine of the
Faith has in the meanwhile gone through your
response and once again has reflected on your
entire doctrinal trial. Even if in specific points
you have given only partially satisfying responses, the Congregation does not now wish to
pursue those points further. It is rather of the
view that in this phase it is more pressing to require you once again to submit your fundamental
stance toward the authentic Magisterium of the
Church to a conscientious examination in light of
the following reflections and to inquire into and
revise your concrete attitude in individual questions as well.
      At the outset of the letter of May 18 of last
year this Congregation summoned you to this in
that it expressed its concern about the relationship between the Magisterium and theologians

and mentioned in this regard the conclusions of the International Theological Commission (cf. *Gregorianum*, 57 [1976], pp. 549–563). In your written response you unfortunately did not deal with the cited thesis 5 of the International Theological Commission, but rather merely delivered a critique of the theological expression "unity of faith and morals" ("unità della fede e dei costumi"), which objectively was out of place.

In your written response you call your love of the Church a "suffering and critical love." On this matter the following passage from the communication of our Congregation on May 18 deserves to be cited: . . . (p. 3). It should be once again stated here that the Congregation in no way doubts your piety and love for the Church.

Rather, it concerns the concrete manner in which you take positions concerning the declaration of the Magisterium of the Church. . . .

The Congregation is of the view that your "critical love" for the Church is not "positive" enough and that your conscious responsibility as a scholar and theologian is not always sufficiently and convincingly expressed, for sometimes you precipitously bring conclusions before the public which are not yet certified in a scholarly manner (e.g., "Responsible Parenthood in Light of Genetics," *Theological Studies, Rivista di Teologia Morale*, and *Theologie der Gegenwart*). Sometimes, although basically agreeing with an expression of the Magisterium, you pick out a peripheral point or a specific theological concept and present it in such a manner that an ambiguous impression is raised and the ecclesial doctrine itself is obscured (e.g., your commentary on *Persona humana* as a "Liber gomorrhianus"). And what is still more questionable is that sometimes you present opinions that are one-sidedly critical or not sufficiently nuanced in widely distributed magazines (e.g., *Famiglia Cristiana*) or in public lectures, with the result that a common sentiment against the Magisterium develops (cf. the International Theological Commission thesis #8, paragraph 1). Such actions visibly disrupt your dialogue with the Magisterium.

The Congregation for the Doctrine of the Faith invites you, therefore, to think over these points, which are of a fundamental nature, and to take them to heart. Then your future service as a theologian and pastor will be a more convincing proof of your love for the Church and your loyalty to the Magisterium. If you wish, this Congregation is obviously prepared to have a clarifying dialogue with you on the questions raised here.

United in Christ, and in the hope that these statements will be received in a proper manner, I greet you.

Franjo Cardinal Seper
Prefect

I look upon this last communication of the Doctrinal Congregation as especially revealing. No open criticism is to be permitted, and critical theologians are to be silenced through doctrinal trials and by their religious superiors if in the smallest matters they think other than what has been expressed by the Magisterium. Thus, not only dissent, but also every critical expression is seen as a punishable action.

(Document 11)
To His Eminence Franjo Cardinal Seper
Prefect of the Doctrinal Congregation
                              Rome, April 29, 1978

Your Eminence,
    I hereby acknowledge the reception of your communication of April 26. I thank you for the warm personal note in your official communication. Certainly I am always prepared to probe my conscience anew in order to better serve the kingdom of God.
    Whoever is committed passionately to the Church and its renewal would rather commit a clear mistake than to be an inert conformist.
    Before God I will not allow myself to complain about the painful experiences with parts of the official Church which preceded the doctrinal trial, accompanied it and intensified themselves in it. They are offset more than a hundred-fold by the love which almost everywhere has been given to me in my apostolate and in my theological work, most especially through the countless men and women who thanked me because they have discovered or returned to the Church. Thanks to the grace of God and to this rich experience of love I emerge for now from these battles without having become despondent or embittered, timid or cynical. However great the temptation might be for me, I have found in my pastoral and human

contacts several persons who have had similar or worse experiences. It is a great miracle of grace if one's love becomes more pure and enthusiastic, not only for the Church in general, but even for all who have precipitated such experiences.

I am thankful for the friendly offer of a dialogue. I hope that you do not misunderstand it as an act of unfriendliness if I do not express such a desire. Indeed, I already had an open and clarifying conversation with Msgr. A. Bovone, for which I was and am very thankful. I also wish to thank Your Eminence for the friendly encounter of January 10th of this year.

Yours in the Lord sincerely,

Bernhard Häring, C.Ss.R.

(Document 12)
Sacred Congregation for the Doctrine of Faith
Prot. N. 13/59

Rome, June 20, 1978

Most Reverend Father Häring,

Thank you very much for your letter of April 30 which was an immediate response to this Congregation's communication of April 26.

In your letter you expressed your willingness to probe your conscience ever anew and also indirectly admit to having committed "clear mistakes." You write then of your experiences and of your efforts for the kingdom of God. From all this your profoundly religious disposition emerges very clearly, which the Congregation also wishes to acknowledge fully.

However, we wish to draw your attention to the main concern of our letter of April 26,

namely, to your basic stance toward the authentic
Magisterium of the Church. In your response you
unfortunately did not delve directly into this, but
rather have been content to take a position concerning individual points of doctrine which were
introduced into our letter only as examples in
order to illustrate your fundamental position on
this point.

You further say that you believe that the offered dialogue is no longer necessary and refer to
the already conducted dialogues with the Cardinal Prefect and the Under Secretary of this Congregation. The referred to conversations, however, did not touch upon the concerns mentioned
in our letter.

Therefore, once again I wish to issue the invitation to you to clarify your fundamental understanding and your attitude as a theologian toward the Magisterium of the Church with the
responsible persons of this Congregation, which,
for example, could take place in autumn after the
holidays.

In the hope that you will accept this offer, I
remain,

Yours in Christ,

Franjo Cardinal Seper
Prefect

(Document 13)
His Eminence Franjo Cardinal Seper
Prefect of the Doctrinal Congregation
Monroe, Michigan, August 3, 1978

Your Eminence,
I wrote my last letter in a state of extreme

exhaustion and profound depression. When you informed me in April that the doctrinal trial would be continued, I lost five and a half pounds in just a few days. (Under my doctor's orders I had to check my weight daily.)

I am now experiencing restful days in the Visitation House of Prayer. In the atmosphere of faith and praise, God has largely freed me of my resentment. I am prepared for a thorough dialogue and I pray and hope that it can take place in an atmosphere of calm and inner peace. Of course the doctrinal trial continues to be a severe burden for me, but I see this burden, which does not come from the Lord himself, as a grace-filled call to the fulfillment of the commandment: "Bear one another's burdens and so you will fulfill the law of Christ" (Gal 6:2). Perhaps God will make our colloquium fruitful for all.

In order to prepare for a fruitful colloquium I would like to make my understanding of the "authentic Magisterium" as clear as possible. Everything that I say here I have written elsewhere in other words. However, a colloquium requires a clear and systematic foundation.

I speak first of all of an official "Magisterium" of the successors of St. Peter and the successors of the apostle in its necessary unity; then of the authentic and inauthentic contribution of theologians.

The Magisterium in the Church coincides with the commission and the grace to preach the Gospel of the living God and of the living Lord to all peoples and cultures in a vital manner. The primary concern of the Magisterium, therefore, cannot be control, but rather constant loyalty in the vital proclamation, which cannot be separated from the witness of life. I recognize, however, the right to the control of orthodox teaching in the Church, even if in my convictions such control—as, for example, in "doctrinal trials"—should be radically subordinated to the mission of a vital proclamation.

I. I believe in an *infallible Magisterium* in the Church, as was determined by the First and Second Vatican Councils in the confrontation between the maximalists and the minimalists.

II. *Non-infallible = a fallible Magisterium:* I hold the division between on the one hand the infallible and on the other the authentic Magisterium to be insufficient and unfelicitous. One could even come to the unhappy idea that with this division the infallible Magisterium need not be considered the authentic Magisterium. It is my conviction that the authenticity of doctrines is guaranteed in the highest degree by the infallible exercise of the Magisterium.

Within the area of the "non-infallible Magisterium" the question about authenticity is a decisive question. Under authenticity I understand precisely what the German phenomenologists understand with the word "echt" (genuine). I propose to distinguish three categories of authenticity ("Echtheit") regarding the exercise of the Magisterium commissioned by Christ:

1. Authentic in every regard:

a) In content and form the statement is a genuine reflection of the Gospel, an expression of creative *fidelity* in the highest degree, and complete openness to the direction of the Holy Spirit by all participants.

b) In complete harmony with the witness of life and the corresponding openness to a synthesis between a constant personal conversion and a constant institutional renewal.

c) Genuine/authentic in the origin of the doctrinal pronouncement and in the carrying out of a doctrinal trial in regard to the purity of motives of all participants: a genuine reflection of the attitude "blessed are the poor in spirit, for they shall see ('know') God."

Genuine/authentic not only by concentrating attention on an isolated text—*textus probantes*—but with a view to the mission of the whole Church, and particularly with the commandment: "be merciful as your heavenly Father" (Lk. 6:36); genuine in its global view, which is so decisive for the carrying out of the mission of evangelization.

d) Genuine/authentic in faith in the Holy Spirit who works in all, through all, and for all; and therefore genuine in the inclusion of the various theological schools and the exclusion of all fanatical "ideological chauvinism" (of one school against others, as so often has been the case in the history of the Church); genuine in the sense of catholicity as it was proclaimed ahead of time in the pentecostal experience: in openness to various cultures and various generations; in patient inclusion of experience and solidary reflection of the entire Church—of all Christianity.

Genuine in the affirmation of that variety without which the diffusion of the Gospel in the whole world would be unthinkable.

e) Genuine in the readiness to live history with the Lord as an Exodus Church, as a Pilgrim Church, in the readiness to admit the limits of knowledge and not to believe that at every moment a finally valid answer can or must be given to all questions.

f) Genuine in the readiness to openly admit earlier errors—and not only those of the dead—including the less than genuine/authentic manner of drawing up doctrinal documents, e.g., the manner in which the declaration of the Holy Office on the Comma Joanneum arose, when every trained exegete could have provided a clear explanation.

2. The grades of imperfection of authenticity in the exercise of the Magisterium when one or many elements indispensable for full authenticity are lacking, of course without any personal or collective guilt, but rather only because of human imperfection which also contaminates the teaching Church in its activity and may in part be rooted in the sins of many;

3. Partially inauthentic manner of teaching and controlling when and insofar as there are direct violations of the qualities of full authenticity laid out in number one;

Several examples for number three: The old situation of the Church in which the "direct power of the Church leaders over all earthly realms" was taught with such solemnity and such emphasis, and the control connected therewith; the solemn magisterial sanctioning of the burning of witches and heretics; the bitter struggle over the temporal state of the Church and the severe disciplinary punishments against those theologians who out of love for the Church expressed their dissent in this regard.

Since theologians are jointly responsible for the less authentic, or indeed inauthentic, manner of teaching, I must on this occasion also raise for myself questions about the authenticity or inauthenticity of the teaching of theologians, or better said, of individual theologians and groups of theologians:

Conditions of authenticity in loyalty in the fulfillment of their teaching mission, and possible sins against it:

a) Theologians must be persons of prayer in the tradition of the prophets of the Old and New Testaments; they must constantly learn prayer anew in the community of the faith and with the "simple" people to whom God has revealed his secrets.

b) They must vigorously and persistently study their whole life long, from time to time burn their lectures or bury them and work them up anew; they must be prepared to learn from others, maintain contact with the entire theological community, especially, with the Holy Scriptures, with the entire tradition of the Church and with the Magisterium; they must learn from the human sciences; for theology is always a triad: to know God in Jesus Christ, to know humanity in

Jesus Christ and in historical reality, and to learn to pray.

3) Theologians, especially those who exercise the official Magisterium, along with their immediate collaborators, constantly must watch over the purity of their motives: "all for the greater honor of God and for the salvation of men and women." They can sin gravely and defame theology through cowardice as well as through arrogance. They can distort the approach to truth for themselves and others by striving for offices and positions or titles of honor, which was so radically forbidden by the Lord. Such sins can be institutionalized, as indeed all sins carry within themselves the tendency to "incarnate" themselves in history. A theologian or group of theologians becomes inauthentic when, rather than suffer for the truth, they allow themselves to be frightened and choose to bury the talents of creative freedom and creative loyalty in favor of "safe" repetition of old formulas.

d) Theologians will become useless and inauthentic not only through cowardice, but also if they allow themselves to become embittered and —instead of proclaiming the good news—struggle for their cause out of resentment and with bitterness. A theologian can likewise betray the Church and truth when he denies his conviction of the truth "out of obedience," just as when he goes his own lonely way in rebellious disobedience and battles embittered (even when such a battle is necessary); for one can be authentic in life, in learning and in teaching only in the peace of Christ.

I would be thankful if all those who take part in the colloquium and all those who in the past have taken part in my doctrinal trial would read and meditate on my reflections in prayer just as I myself wrote them after long prayer.

In peace of Christ I remain, sincerely,

Bernhard Häring, C.Ss.R.

(Document 14)
Sacred Congregation for the
    Doctrine of the Faith
Prot. N. 13/59

Rome, October 12, 1978

Most Reverend Father Häring,

Your two letters of July 12 and August 3 of this year have arrived here in the Congregation for the Doctrine of the Faith. You spoke in them of the impression which the previous communications of this Congregation made upon you and of their negative effect upon your health.

Be assured that the Doctrinal Congregation has always followed with concern the condition of your health and wishes you with all its heart a definitive stabilization of your health. The colloquium with the responsible persons of this Congregation to which you have been invited, however, should in its nature not be a reason for concern or a worsening of your health, especially since such a dialogue, such a clarifying colloquium has time and again been desired by many theologians.

There seems to be in this concrete case much

more a misunderstanding about the theme and the goal of the planned colloquium. Therefore I wish once again to be precise about this: Several elements of your concrete/practical attitude in regard to the statements of the Magisterium of the Church are to be discussed and clarified that you might ever better realize precisely that which you demand in your last letter from theologians: "They must be ready to learn from others, remain in contact with the entire theological community, especially with the Holy Scriptures, with the entire tradition of the Church and with the Magisterium" (p. 2).

Unfortunately in view of the *Sede vacante* [there was no pope at the time] the planned colloquium cannot at the moment take place. You will certainly understand this and wait in inner calm until the matter can be taken up again.

In the meanwhile I recommend myself and above all the entire Church to your prayers and I remain,

United in the Lord,
Jerome Hamer, O.P.

I am convinced that the responsible persons of the Doctrinal Congregation were always honestly interested in my health. However, in such a hard and persistent doctrinal trial about my book on the "healing ministry" they could also have attended more to the section on the psychosomatic influence of continued tension in a struggle against the metasticizing of cancer. Of course, the Doctrinal Congregation did not wish to damage my health.

(Document 15)
Sacred Congregation for the
    Doctrine of the Faith
Prot. N. 13/59

Rome, February 1, 1979

Most Reverend Father Häring,
    On October 12th of last year we informed
you that the planned colloquium on several elements of your concrete/practical attitude in regard to the statements of the Magisterium of the
Church could not take place that time. We would
now like to take that matter up again and ask you
to make yourself available for the colloquium on
Tuesday, February 27, at 10 a.m. here in the
Congregation.
    In the hope that the specified appointment is
possible for you, I recommend myself to your
prayers and greet you with friendship,
        United in the Lord,

Franjo Cardinal Seper
Prefect

    The last communication to me from the Doctrinal
Congregation came on April 2, 1979 as an Easter greeting
from Cardinal Seper.

(Document 16)
Sacred Congregation for the
    Doctrine of the Faith
Prot. N. 13/59

April 2, 1979

Most Reverend Father,

On the occasion of the meeting on February 27 this Congregation expressed its reserve and concern which had been called forth by several of your statements concerning certain doctrines, especially in regard to the doctrine of the Magisterium.

The approaching Easter feast gives me the opportunity at the same time to express with the Christian wish of peace the confidence that you will adhere to the admonitions of this Congregation to work together with the Magisterium for a better and more precise understanding of the teaching presented by the Church. The Congregation would like to hope that its trust will find confirmation in the second volume of *Free and Faithful in Christ* in which, as is evident from the first volume, the problems of sexuality will be treated, which were a basis for the special intervention of this Congregation.

Yours very sincerely,

Franjo Cardinal Seper
Prefect

This is the last written communication which I have received from the Doctrinal Congregation. I have never been informed that the doctrinal trial against me has come to a close.

How did the colloquium on February 27, 1979, go?

I think that several things are clear from the letter of April 2. I came to the "closing colloquium" referred to in an extremely bad state of health. Cardinal Seper was a model of friendliness. However, Archbishop Hamer and, if in a somewhat less severe tone, Msgr. Bovone came at me with severe censures. They most of all concerned the fact that while a doctrinal trial was going on against me I had dared publicly to criticize their document *Persona humana*, concerning questions of sexual morality. I was not in condition to respond sensibly since my head was in a whirl. I turned to Cardinal Seper and said that I intended to publish this documentation. He responded with great calm: "You may do so!"

Things were spinning around me and I left the "palace of the Holy Office" feeling very ill. However, inwardly I was happy that I had not succumbed to servility.

During the long period of this doctrinal trial did you have no personal contact with the top leadership of the Doctrinal Congregation?

In the beginning of 1978, shortly after my return following the third operation on my throat, the then Under-Secretary, Msgr. Alberto Bovone, visited me. He is at present the Secretary of the Doctrinal Congregation and an Archbishop. He brought me the greetings of Cardinal Seper and his apology that unfortunately other obligations had prevented him from visiting me in the hospital, as had been planned and desired by the Cardinal of the Doctrinal Congregation. I was somewhat reserved partly because of the doctrinal trial, but also because I was once again just learning to speak. Msgr. Bovone invited me in the name of the cardinals to a friendly visit in the palace of the Holy Office. My first reaction was to decline with the excuse of my handicap. But I soon had to admit to myself that this really contradicted my desire for non-violence. And so I accepted the invitation. On the day that the visit took place I was in better health and could again to a certain extent speak. The conversation was friendly, without admonishments.

Do you see a connection between the strong attack on you in the Osservatore Romano *on its front page of January 2/3, 1975, and your doctrinal trial?*

That article was doubtless the strongest attack against me from the Vatican side. And I certainly had not "deserved" this attack. On December 27, 1974, the journalist F. De Sanctis published an article in which he accused Pope Paul VI of lacking coherence in ecumenical questions. I complained about this to one of his colleagues. Thereupon De Sanctis telephoned me in order to justify himself. In the course of the conversation I remarked that a pope is dependent upon his collaborators and that not all texts can come out equally felicitously. From this De Sanctis constructed an interview—unauthorized and without asking me—with the title: "Pope Paul VI cannot always say what he wishes." Thereupon on January 2 a sharp article appeared on the front page of the *Osservatore Romano* in which it said that I had maintained that not all of the speeches by the pope would be written by him. A few days later I was requested to appear before Archbishop Augustin Mayer, at that time the Secretary of the Congregation for Religious. He carried out, indeed more than carried out, his obligation to deliver a stern admonition before he allowed me to speak. Thereupon I explained the matter in a factual letter to the Cardinal Secretary of State Villot. Villot responded in a friendly manner. With this the matter appeared to be ended. On this occasion humble apologies were expected of me, but no one apologized for having condemned me without first hearing me.

After all of your experiences, what reforms of the Doctrinal Congregation would you suggest?

When Cardinal Frings said in St. Peter's before the whole assembly of the Council that the Holy Office was a scandal for all Christendom, the English-speaking journalists pressed around me at the following press conference, asking what reforms I would suggest. I answered with a single word—"discontinuity"—but I did not mean, as the large newspapers of many countries insisted, simply its elimination. I meant then, and still mean today, that a temporary interruption is needed in order to gain perspective on the past, to be able to evaluate it thoroughly and work out its implications.

Moreover, a new wine needs new wine skins. Good intentions and admonishment alone do not help in the long term. New structures are needed, and men and women who, so to speak, come from the front ranks of pastoral work and who wish to return there. A constant flow of new blood is needed. Certain things simply must not exist anymore. I name only one: had the anonymous author of the accusing document against me been forced to state it publicly and face me, he would not have allowed himself to use such sloppy language.

A credible proclamation and a witness to the faith are fundamental for the maintenance of a pure faith. Hence, I believe that for such an institution women and men who have shown themselves as proclaimers and witnesses of the faith are above all necessary. Does it still need to be said that such an institution needs women and men from all the different significant theological schools and various cultures?

Have you had no further complaints or difficulties from Vatican agencies since 1979?

From 1979 to 1982 I was very ill and for the most part out of the sight of Rome. In 1982/83 a dark cloud again appeared. For the twenty-fifth anniversary of the Academia Alfonsiana I wrote in *Studia Moralia* (#20, 1982, pp. 29–66) an article with the title "Twenty-five Years of Sexual Ethics." On December 20, 1982, the Congregation of Studies sent to the Academia Alfonsiana, through the Grand Chancellor of the Lateran University, Cardinal Ugo Poletti, a long, devastating review of my article, which obviously was aimed not only at me but also at the Academia Alfonsiana. In it was the exact same language, the exact same jargon, the exact same insinuations as in the annex of my doctrinal trial.

I took up the battle with my own hands and vigorously demanded a confrontation with the "expert." When no response was forthcoming, I personally spoke out. I wrote a detailed analysis about the style of the "expert" who mixed together insinuations and cries of alarm. Shortly thereafter there appeared in *Osservatore Romano* a highly laudatory review of the Italian edition of my three-volume work *Free and Faithful in Christ*. The matter was clarified, and our relations with the Congregation of Studies, it appears to me, can be described as good. Hence, I do not wish to publish here any documentations on this problem. The matter is finished. It is perhaps worth mentioning that the "expert" who had written the review for the Congregation of Studies argued that a return to an Augustinian understanding of sexual morality was desirable. I do not know his name.

8

CONTEMPORARY QUESTIONS

Cardinal Siri was one of those who said of persons with AIDS: "God has punished you!" What do you think about this?

Thank God that such judgments are the exception in the Church today. Pope John Paul II has spoken in a completely different way, full of sympathy, without any tone of judgment.

We are all dependent upon God's mercy, on God's healing love. Certainly now and again the consequences of our own sins and the sins of others do afflict us simply through a chain reaction. That is part of the reality of an incomplete creation. Occasionally nature strikes back. However, God does not strike back. That is what the suffering of the non-violent servant of God on the cross tells us. He did not answer insult with insult. He expressly said to us: "I have not come to judge, but to heal." Jesus himself asks of these judging men of the Church: "Have you not also sinned, perhaps even more severely?" Whoever self-righteously judges others must hear the Lord say to them: "Do not think that those . . . were greater sinners than others! No! If you do not repent, you too will perish"

189

(Lk 13:3–5). Such a judge destroys himself. And if such a judge is one day himself struck with severe suffering, he must ask himself the question: "For what sins has God sent me this punishment?"

There is still always the tendency to condemn more severely defects in the area of sexual morality than, for example, sins against justice and peace or indeed the sin of self-righteousness. In addition, it should be remembered that some of those who are infected with AIDS are so without any sins against chastity, e.g., through blood transfusions.

Those infected with AIDS have, as do all the ill, the right to receive our sympathy, and, as far as is possible, also our support. And by no means may we treat these human beings as branded outcasts. There must be a balance between the mandatory or voluntary measures taken to avoid infecting others and, on the other hand, unnecessarily burdening or isolating those who are infected.

I also find it severe when casuists quickly leap to the position that those who are infected with AIDS must embrace total abstinence in marriage. It is clear to me that premarital chastity, the avoidance of all promiscuity and absolute marital faithfulness are critically decisive presuppositions for overcoming AIDS. However, to demand of those spouses who are infected with AIDS that they observe absolute continence and the strict prohibition of the use of condoms can have painful consequences. While it is clear that there should be a warning against trusting condoms in homosexual intercourse—in the anal sexual act condoms can easily be torn. But it is quite different with normal marital intercourse. One should leave room in these delicate questions for the married couple to decide for themselves.

There are also priests who have contracted AIDS. For the sake of avoiding difficulties, shouldn't these cases be kept absolutely secret?

In all cases one should not publicly expose those who are sick with AIDS. However, to give the impression that there are no priests who have contracted something of this sort would be dishonest. For a long time I corresponded with a respected priest, willing to sacrifice, who himself had contracted AIDS. He had opened himself in faith to the meaning of suffering and before his death, completely on his own, requested his bishop to clearly state at his burial, or in some other manner, that he died as a consequence of AIDS. Likewise another priest, who on his own contacted me and continued his contact, died in model devotion and great trust in God. I believe that it is good to speak of these things, free from all judgment, so that other AIDS patients, or others severely stricken, with cancer for example, can take courage.

As one who has lost his voice box, I have been in touch with many others with the same affliction. Most of them were chain smokers. Time and again one comes up against the painful question: "Why did the Creator punish me so severely?" At the beginning of an in-depth conversation I note that I have had the same affliction without ever having smoked, and that indeed there are many smokers who never have cancer. And then, in view of the book of Job and other parts of the Bible it is clear that it is right to say: Let us put the guilt questions behind us; let us judge neither others nor ourselves into perdition! Let us in view of the cross give suffering the correct meaning, regardless of how it came to us. And even if we do have accusations to make against ourselves, let us turn repentantly, but also with complete trust, to God. And praise him for his mercy and thank him that our suffering attained an ultimate meaning from the suffering of Christ.

In Italy there are bishops, priests and a growing number of laity who are refusing to pay that part of their taxes which will be used for armaments. What do you think about this?

To my knowledge it was Bishop Hunthausen from Seattle in America who was the first bishop to keep back a percentage of his taxes which would go for armaments. He did not do that secretly, in order to lessen his taxes, but rather with a public declaration of the reasons for his actions. He belongs to the many bishops who are convinced that under present conditions war, and even the preparation for war, must be outlawed. There is another way: the alternative of non-violent defense as part of a more comprehensive plan in which education and politics are used in an effort to strive toward the goal of a non-violent world culture.

In Italy the number of bishops and priests who hold the same view is increasing steadily. Our goal is to follow up such a conscientious objection with a genuinely democratic law which grants every citizen the right to declare at the beginning of every calendar year whether his or her portion of taxes should be used for the military or rather for the development of a non-violent defense. In this connection we are also working for the goal that every young man can decide in complete freedom whether he wishes to fulfill his period of public service in the old defense system, or rather in the service of a spiritual, strategic and tactical preparation of a socially non-violent defense. In this case women also can present themselves for a period of public service in the furtherance of a non-violent world culture and the development of a non-violent defense. With this a decisive step toward a genuine democracy will have been taken.

As long as our governments still wish to build their defense behind the "nuclear shield," the concept of democracy is very fragile, indeed, emptied of meaning. What meaning does it have for us to elect party representatives if "in a crisis" the Secretary General in Moscow or the President of the United States, after consulting only with a few generals, can make the decision for nuclear war. Such a decision could all too easily lead to the annihilation of all life on our planet! Against such eventualities we must defend ourselves, being prepared to defend the fundamental rights of all human beings through non-violent means. The refusal to pay taxes and/or serve in the military for reasons of conscience is only a single step toward a more comprehensive goal.

I maintain that this kind of conscientious objection as an expression of a non-violent protest against the arms trade and armament industries and as a democratic step toward a purely non-violent dissent, is meaningful and irreproachable. The treasury is refused nothing, and no personal advantage is sought. The corresponding sum will be transferred to a fund, which in Italy can be put at the disposal of the President with the aim of research for the development of a non-violent defense and similar projects. That bishops as well as a portion of the clergy are also participating in this is particularly gratifying.

Can one today, in view of the horrifying weapons systems and especially the danger of nuclear escalation, still maintain the theory of "a just war"?

The pastoral letter of the American bishops on the challenge of peace, after a careful analysis of the conditions for a just war, comes to the enlightening conclusion that today one can no longer imagine a just war; for the consequences of a war between heavily armed great powers make the principle of proportionality unthinkable: The injuries of a moral and material nature, the loss of life, would be so great that the advantages sought hardly weigh in the balance. Furthermore, in modern warfare the soldiers are no longer the main victims. The proportion of the killed and wounded from the civilian population, even in the Korean War, was many times that of the fallen soldiers.

Erasmus of Rotterdam showed in his book *Querela pacis* that practically none of the wars known to him could be designated as just, according to the measures set up by a sound theology. True freedom and justice in any case cannot be defended by a war. It is my firm conviction, which I attempted to spell out in my book *The Healing Power of Peace and Nonviolence* (New York: Paulist Press, 1986), that there is an alternative which in fact serves the freedom and justice for all. It is precisely the social non-violent defense, which is completely unthinkable without a sense of justice for all and a world-wide solidarity. If in the age of nuclear weapons, capable of global destruction, we do not learn a radical transformation and conversion to non-violence, and with that the vigorous commitment to non-violence and a non-violent love which changes enemies into friends, then the chances for humanity are poor. Even poorer will be the credibility of the Church. What shall we say of a Church which intensifies the prohibition of artificial birth control as absolute and without exception and attempts to enforce it with all conceivable sanctions, while at the same time in the face of the danger of nuclear escalation interprets the prohibition to kill so laxly that the idea of a just war can still be retained?

What does peace mean in a biblically grounded moral theology?

Forty years ago we accepted it as normal that the only discussion of peace in the handbooks of moral theology was a chapter with the title "Concerning the State's Right to War." Now moral theology, which has been biblically renewed and is attentive to the signs of the times, treats the topic of peace in a central manner, as a precious gift and most pressing task for all Christians, and of course most especially for those who bear political responsibility.

In the view of the Hebrew Bible, peace is the well-being that is wished and offered by God for the whole people, for all human beings. It is the "yes" to together-ness, to solidarity, to an always increasing mutuality. Peace also includes physical well-being, which presumes healthy and health-bringing human relationships in the family, in the community, in the entire people.

Irreconcilability, grudges and hate are the enemies of peace, the enemies of humanity. The divine gift of peace, as it was fully revealed in Jesus Christ, embraces an untiring love which turns enemies into friends, which seeks to imitate the all-merciful God and Savior. It is the touch-stone of the authenticity of the love of God and the follow-ing of Christ.

There is no Gospel other than that of peace. There-fore there can be no genuinely Christian morality as long as the message of peace is not present everywhere and pervasive in all things.

What is the relationship between the formation of an ecological consciousness, a conscience sensitive to the Gos-pel, and a morality of peace?

The great physicist, philosopher and peace-researcher, Carl Friedrich von Weizsäcker, called the churches to a great Peace Council. The expression "Council" should remind us that Christ, our peace, had given the Church above all the task to witness to and proclaim peace and to encourage all men and women of good will to peace and to everything which leads to peace. Had the Gospel and its evangelical attitude of a readiness and striving for peace remained vital in Christendom, the divisions and hostilities between the parts of Christendom, which are profound, painful and endlessly injurious for all humankind, would not have arisen. Thus, it appears to lie in the logic of the Gospel that Christendom should come together to a Peace Council both for its own unity and to fulfill its world mission. Such a Council would be an opportunity jointly to repent for our sins against peace and to turn back to the Lord, who is our peace. In the question of peace we not only are dealing with the survival of humanity, but also with the credibility and the future of Christendom.

The term "Peace Council" appears to me to be completely appropriate. However, so as not to waste time disputing what to call it, any other term would also be acceptable if it can communicate meaningfully the significance and central task of such an event. Thus, one speaks now of a world assembly with three themes which condition and develop each other: 1. Peace in the fullest sense; the spread of peace throughout the nations. 2. Peace as the fruit and work of justice, the peace of the rich with the poor, the first and second worlds with the third world. 3. Peace with the creation which has been entrusted to us by God. The latter is the same as a deeply rooted ecological consciousness and conscience.

*How do non-violence and a non-violent world culture,
which you emphasize so greatly, fit together with justice
and an ecological conscience?*

I see this in a way very similar to Gustavo Gutiérrez,
who expresses it with the key concept of the experience of
gratuity.

As long as and insofar as men and women experience
and respect themselves, each other, and all creation as a
gift of God, then for them the earth is a paradise. Non-violence, peace, justice and a joyful solidarity will blossom
forth. Humanity, however, absorbed death and drove itself out of paradise when it "ate from the forbidden tree."
What does that mean? Being concerned only with themselves individually, they appropriate to themselves what
God the Creator had created as a gift for all. They steal the
gift and respect from God. What, according to God's plan,
should unite humanity, now divides them. Whereas, when
they eat their bread, enjoy the fruit of the earth jointly for
one another and with one another, there is peace, gratitude, true worship of God. Where, however, individual
and collective self-seeking dominate, men and women lose
the sense that all things, including their own existence,
have been given to them. They see in others rivals and
they strike out at otherness. They impoverish others mis-
erably and thereby also contaminate others and their envi-
ronment. The entire creation sighs and groans in this condition of greed.

The original state willed by God, between a man and
woman, Adam and Eve, is the experience of joy in one
another, the experience that they are given by God to one
another precisely in their otherness and complementarity.

Every man should experience himself as "Theodor" (God's gift), and every woman as "Dorothee" (the gift of God). However, as soon as men and women contaminate each other with ingratitude, with the refusal to respect all creation as a gift of God to them and to everyone, they begin to blame each other. While in God's original plan Adam rejoiced in Eve, whom God created out of the innermost yearning of his heart ("out of his rib"), now a contemptuous casting of blame has taken the upper hand. Sin strikes back and springs out in the demand of the man to dominate the woman, to treat her as a thing, as if she were not a gift of God, equal to him. With the loss of the core experience of gratitude all the fundamental relationships among human beings, among the various groups, and between humanity and the rest of creation are distorted in the most profound manner. Paradise has become a battlefield with thorns and thistles, with poisoned human relations. The first chapters of the book of Genesis, up to the story of the flood, are a presentation of this experience in gripping imagery.

Christ, the non-violent servant of God receives his human nature, his solidarity with all humankind, including his corporeality, completely as a gift. He also views all of us sinners as a gift: "Behold, here am I and the children whom God has given me" (Heb 2:13). "You have prepared a body for me. . . . behold, I come to do your will" (Heb 10:5–7).

Only a theology which justifies wars and is alienated from the Gospel of peace could misinterpret the redemption as a sacrificial work to assuage a God filled with revengeful righteousness. Thus also the very heart of the eucharist, the celebration of the world and the constantly renewed commitment to the covenant of peace, would be largely lost.

Within the perspective of peace and non-violence I see things in this way. On the cross Jesus, our peace, gave back his entire human existence, which was united with divinity, as a gift to the Father. In unconditional love he overcame all enmity in the power of the Holy Spirit, who is the eternally proceeding event of the mutual love given and received between the Father and the Son. In the eucharist Jesus is not only "substantially" present; he is also present completely as the gift for us from the Father and to the Father in the same power of the Holy Spirit as in the Easter mystery of death and resurrection. He gives himself to us in the power of the same Holy Spirit. At the same time he gives us the Holy Spirit so that we may become completely a gift for God the Father and for our fellow human beings, open to a healing, saving love which overcomes all enmities, open to the Gospel of peace.

Jesus gives himself in the eucharist under the form of the most fundamental gifts of the earth, bread and wine, so that we in turn can perceive, respect and use everything as a gift of God in a redeemed, healing mutuality. Thus, we celebrate in the eucharist the peace Gospel and we experience the *paraklesis*, the divine enabling and encouraging of us to be children of God and evermore effective in the service of the Gospel of peace. It is precisely this Gospel of peace, which we experience as the highest form of gratuitousness, that makes us into servants of peace and at the same time apostles of a renewed ecological consciousness.

If I have understood you correctly, the question of the role of women in marriage and family, in Church and the

*world, is at the very center of the Gospel of peace and
redemption.*

Absolutely! This "man's church" must think very seriously about this. The one-sided domination of the man is a
central expression of the sinful Fall and a constant new
source of the violence which poisons the world. Through
the course of the centuries the Church has acknowledged
Mary as the greatest gift of God—and that has kept it away
from many erroneous paths. However, the men in leading
positions in the Church in many respects have often not
acknowledged either the otherness or the equal rights of
women. Women were praised for their willingness to
serve, but men have not acknowledged them as a model
for their own position as "servant." There has been talk of
the "feminine" and sexuality without permitting the
women of the Church to speak their own word openly, to
make their own contribution. Unfortunately, it is certainly
true that women are not heard in the Church.

*Do you also believe that the ordained priesthood can
and should also be open to women?*

Here and now I do not place a priority on this question. It does not appear to me that the time has yet arrived
in which we could reflect or dispute this issue in complete
calmness and peace. The Church is still too clericalized to
be able to guarantee a genuine place for women in the
priestly office. In addition, the rejection of the ordination
of women in the Orthodox Churches is almost universal,
and indeed very emphatic. I do not believe that this is an
expression of a contempt or hostility toward women. One
should remember how respected the pastor's wife is in the

Orthodox Churches. The Orthodox are also broadly prepared to grant women the ordination to the diaconate and
a corresponding role in their churches. Moreover, since
they never had a central church-leadership comparable to
the Roman Curia, and, given their understanding of the
Church, never wanted one, they find it extraordinarily
difficult to change the church order and tradition which
has been in place since time immemorial. Since the Roman
Catholic Church is so near to the Orthodox Churches and
has again drawn even closer ecumenically, the ordination
of women at this moment should simply be put off. In the
meanwhile the Reformation churches and the Anglican
family of churches are contributing their experiences,
which according to the judgment of many are very positive and can become still more positive.

In my opinion the following steps can and must be
initiated without delay. The laity in general, and in this
most especially the women, should have a complete and
full right to speak and participate in decisions in decision-
making bodies on all levels, since almost every decision
affects women as much as men. We are concerned here,
therefore, with a pressing need for declericalization.

Women, including significant representatives of femi-
nist theology, should be adequately represented even in
the Doctrinal Congregation and in all theological commissions of a lower level. The men in the leading positions in
the Church should make it clear that they are not seeking
domination, which will injure women, but rather are reflecting a sensitivity for a long, unquestioned tradition.

Women themselves and womanliness must belong to
and be brought into all reflections about sexual morality in
a totally new manner. For it cannot be denied that from
the time of Gregory of Nyssa, through Augustine and
Thomas, to the encyclical *Casti connubii* and up to the

present the celibate male church has heard only those women who were yes-sayers, and infrequently at that.

Would then the official Church have to undertake a very serious penitential analysis of this history and also humbly ask women for pardon?

I believe that this is true not only for the highly placed officials, but also for us theologians. In the course of history and even to this very day we theologians have made statements about women and their place in the Church and world which should make us blush. There is no basis or room for triumphalism. Statements like: "The Church has always defended the dignity and equality of women," simply are not possible. Certainly there were men who in part had done so, but they had to pay a price for it, or were not even heard. There have also been some thoroughly praiseworthy steps forward taken. I refer to the declaration of St. Teresa of Avila and St. Catherine of Siena as Doctors of the Church by Paul VI. This fact has perhaps not been sufficiently appreciated. But one must remember how even today religious women and women's orders have been treated like minors, and often in an overbearing manner. Even during the Second Vatican Council it was not possible to include religious women in the conciliar commission for religious. The president of the conciliar commission responded to such petitions that one could perhaps consider this in a Third or Fourth Vatican Council —being completely convinced that it was out of the question in a Second Vatican Council.

The major seminaries in Rome were until the time of the Council a sad symbol. In Rome, and elsewhere, seminarians (candidates for the priesthood) were not allowed to receive visits from their blood sisters. They were not allowed to visit their fathers and mothers together. Religious nuns were also not to be present in the seminary, not even to care for the sick—all with a view of an "asexual" education for celibacy. Churchmen (many!) similarly believed that religious women for the sake of their virginity had as much as possible to forget their femaleness, their femininity, instead of integrating it in a healthy manner.

Msgr. Landucci, the Rector of the major Roman seminary for many years, described this systematic education for celibacy in an asexual manner in a book which he entitled: "Modern Seminary Education." Before the Council Landucci was very influential in the Italian episcopacy, as well as among those who were resistant after the Council. A newspaper of an Italian workers' union printed some typical pages from the book, without commentary, in order to make the Roman seminary education laughable.

Although this excess should not be caricatured, we cannot afford to ignore it today when we must deal with a new wave of sexual rigorism among those making a career in the Church. These matters should be spelled out by name since it is precisely from these circles which insist that the crisis of celibacy is only the result of the Second Vatican Council and progressive theologians. I myself have been approached for therapy by former seminarians and by priests who have not come through such an education without neuroses.

In your opinion has the celibate male church ever correctly grasped and presented the meaning and goal of human sexuality?

Gregory of Nazianzus—in distinction to Gregory of Nyssa—can be named as one bishop and Doctor of the

Church who has correctly and felicitously presented the biblical view. In songs he praises the value of marriage, concretely referring to the tender marital love of his mother through which she brought her husband (Gregory's father) to the faith and enriched him with those virtues which made him a model bishop. Here then is a case of a married bishop for whom marital love understood in a genuinely Christian way became a path to salvation. Gregory also spoke in a similar manner on the occasion of the marriage of one of his sisters when he composed a beautiful poem to married love. In the Orthodox Churches this spirit has time and again found outstanding representatives.

In the Western Church the otherwise gigantic and genial Augustine turned out to be a major liability. According to him—similar to the thought of Gregory of Nyssa—God's original plan was for an asexual humanity which would propagate by a purely spiritual act. According to Augustine sexuality belongs to the "second plan of creation" and carries with it a character of punishment. The marital act as a sexual act has, according to him, something degrading in it which can be excused only through the express purpose of conception. In comparison to Augustine, Thomas Aquinas is progressive, but he is still largely a prisoner of that tradition.

The encyclical *Casti connubii* of Pius XI follows completely in the Augustinian tradition. Nevertheless, in the course of a long history there have always also been other more healthy traditions. I think that, for example, the German and likewise the French episcopacy in the course of the last decade have given some very helpful directions for a correct understanding. The married laity have collaborated with them in a fruitful manner. However, the question remains: must not the Church, which is led by men, if it speaks in the future on questions of sexuality, also give the voice of women a place in a completely new and systematic manner? Above all, there must be a clearer distinction between the chastity characterized by the continence of those who wish to live as celibates for the sake of the Kingdom of God and a marital chastity which is characterized by two becoming one in a loving manner. Today in the Church it appears to me that the writings of the laity, women and men, on sexuality are read more than the writings of celibate men who simply repeat the old formulas.

Once again there are no grounds here for triumphalism. What is needed is a serious effort toward conversion. However, for the sake of correctness, it should also be noted that since the first centuries the Church has fought a difficult battle against anti-sexual traditions like Manichaeism and Gnosticism and in this defended the value of human sexuality.

Can there be a genuine "yes" to the single vocations without an inner acceptance of one's own sexuality?

The choice of a single or unmarried life for the sake of the Kingdom of God unconditionally presumes a high esteem for the married path. Hostility toward the body, and especially misogyny, would totally devalue celibacy and make a healthy perseverance in an unmarried life thus chosen impossible. However, an initial embarrassment about one's sexuality can under certain circumstances be overcome by an authentic new perspective, and wounds can be healed. Whoever has found his way through such a crisis of growth can also be of the most help to others.

Please allow me an indiscreet question. Has celibacy been a sacrifice for you? Has it been a heavy burden?

I want to answer that question straightforwardly. In my decision for the priesthood and the religious life it was not an easy sacrifice. At home I experienced a loving marriage and a happy family. My parents not only loved and respected each other into old age, they also remained "in love" with one another. As a young man I could very easily imagine what a happy marriage with an intelligent, noble and beautiful woman would be like for me. I was very open to affection and was not blind when an attractive girl had an eye for me. Why should one deny this? It is part of being a normal human being. I have never suffered from misogyny or similar feelings. Precisely because I valued highly the other way, that of marriage, the choice of unmarried chastity for the sake of the Kingdom of Heaven was for me, as for most, a sacrifice, a renunciation deeply felt. It was meaningful only in view of a completely free availability for the work of the Gospel, for love precisely for the unloved and troubled.

I always saw in my celibacy an encouragement for those who for different reasons have remained unmarried against their own will, as well as for the divorced who cannot marry again. To my joy and happiness my celibacy has had no interruption because I had discovered its meaning. It was also clear to me, however, and I understand it much better today than I did at the beginning, that the support of a community and friendship is needed if one is to live unmarried without becoming unnaturally twisted. Why should I not speak of the fact that there were moments for me when I was gripped with a kind of envy as I met friends of my youth with their happy wives and lovely children. Nevertheless, such encounters helped me every time to understand better my own vocation and its beauty, to be thankful for the great amount of love and gratitude which I have experienced everywhere from many men and women. I mention only as an example that some African bishop or theologian would write to me: "Your son Albert, your son Peter. . . ."

The decisive thing in celibacy is that one remains capable of love and gratitude. If, for example, one experiences the beginning of an infatuation, one must make a sober distinction between such infatuation and one's fundamental decision, which hopefully emerges confirmed. Sour "old maids" and sour, unfeeling "old bachelors" certainly have nothing to do with a genuine celibacy. The inner source of power of a freely lived celibacy is the joy in the Lord and the accomplishment of his love for men and women, above all the unloved.

Do you believe that the historically developed linkage between celibacy and admission to the priesthood must also remain intact today?

I could imagine that many married men from many countries could be good and worthy priests. I have personally come to know a large number of married Orthodox priests and exemplary Protestant pastors. I have often been a guest in Protestant pastors' homes. I look with admiration at many of them. I believe that we must revise a historically conditioned concept of "complete chastity" to overcome a psychological barrier to the ordination of married men.

As I wrote the book *The Law of Christ*, the chapter on married and unmarried chastity pleased my publisher Dr. Erich Wewel, and he read it out loud to his noble wife. When she heard that I reserved the concept "complete

chastity" for the unmarried state, she remarked: "But Erich, do not we also as married people try to live chastity
completely?" My publisher related this to me, whereupon
I immediately changed the vocabulary. No one of us can
maintain that we are absolutely complete in chastity, even
when we are completely continent. Is it really fulfilled
completely by love? Does it give love free rein? In the best
of cases, we are simply on the way. However, young men
and women who are married are likewise on the way. I
dare say that many married people are more clearly and
definitely on the way to a genuine married chastity than
are some celibates to a genuinely single or solitary chastity. Only if one narrowly identifies chastity with continence can the concept "complete chastity" be reserved
for the unmarried.

Married people are called to holiness just as we unmarried are, and often follow their vocation even better
than we follow our paths. All this must be said expressly in
order to discuss objectively the question of the ordination
of reliable married men, which is so burning today.

Christ called married men to be apostles, and according to the statement of Paul, Peter took his wife with him
on missionary journeys. That did not detract from his devotion to his apostolic office.

Now, to speak directly about this matter concerning
which I have reflected a great deal and have sought advice
from many: the present situation in the "Latin" Church
(Western-Roman Church) is in my opinion untenable. In
broad portions of the Church we have a great lack of authentic vocations to celibacy. For this reason there exists
in many places a tendency to ordain young men who are
not suitable in all respects for pastoral life and often also
not for the observance of celibacy.

A large portion of Catholics have no regular opportunities to join in the celebration of the eucharist and the reception of the sacraments, including the sacrament of the dying. The right to a regular participation in the eucharist comes from the solemn testament, the act of empowerment of Jesus: "Do this in my memory. Take and eat this *all of you!*" The Church interprets this expressly in a way that if at all possible everyone must participate in the mass every Sunday and Holy Day. On the other hand, the admission of only the unmarried to the priesthood is a purely human tradition. But it must be clear that in cases of conflict the divine act of empowerment has to have priority.

In today's society there is a strong sensitivity for the right to marry as a fundamental right, above all because the unmarried who are not integrated into a family feel themselves isolated in the great mass of the living. Being single for the sake of the Kingdom of Heaven can with the grace of God be relatively easily realized in a religious community or a similar community of priests. The Eastern Church, which has ordained and still ordains married men with stable family relations, has thereby always had outstanding vocations to the priestly state. They would also not fail in the Western Church if there were more trust in the working of the Holy Spirit than in legal regulations.

I do not wish to be misunderstood to be saying that now diocesan priests should be in the marriage market. I am pleading for an understanding for those who are not able to manage celibacy. My main concern, however, is that the Western Church may not violate the right to a regular participation in the eucharist of a large part, indeed, even the majority of the faithful, for the sake of a law of celibacy based on this human tradition and legal structure. The following also should be noted: if one presents

celibacy as fundamentally meaningless, then one makes
the admission of married men to the priesthood unnecessarily difficult. I would therefore like to expressly emphasize the value of the charism of celibacy.

In Africa I have time and again had the opportunity to
know and admire wonderful catechists and their wives.
What a spirit of faith and sacrifice! What human warmth
with their fellow believers! Now they—thank God—at
least can celebrate the liturgy of the Word, and most can
also celebrate communion. But why should these men
have to travel fifty and more kilometers in order to pick up
consecrated hosts? Why should they be forbidden to
speak the words of consecration only because they have a
wife and family (also prepared for sacrifice)?

*Can one then still teach that the unmarried state is
higher than the married state?*

I presume that this manner of speaking comes from
the concept of the classes in the Middle Ages. Among the
disciples of Christ such a concept was unknown. Before
God we are all sisters and brothers. We are all fully and
completely called to holiness and to an inner love of God. I
believe, however, that celibacy for the sake of the kingdom of God is a gift of the Holy Spirit, a charism in which
those who are called may not take any pride. In a world
which stands in danger of admitting only a this-worldli-
ness, it has a certain urgency, and under certain circumstances even a priority. But this may not be expressed by
the terms "higher-lower."

I treasure my vocation. But it would be crazy to think
that because of my vocation I stood higher than, for example, my parents, who obviously made more sacrifices than
I have. It is a matter of a difference of the gift of the Spirit

and vocation. But no one can boast because of his state in life!

I have seen in a number of your publications that you are very involved in "houses of prayer." Why is that so?

My main concern was to learn to "pray in spirit and in truth," together with kindred souls to learn to love Jesus ever more, and thereby to cultivate the worship of God in the spirit and in truth above all. I suggested these ideas especially immediately after the Council to several general chapters of women and men religious in order to prevent an enthusiasm for modernization which is too horizontal. The ideas were taken up most of all by women's orders involved in the apostolic life and creatively realized. A leitmotif always was: the integration of faith and life, the integration of prayer in the spirit and in the truth, along with the experience of community.

For me, however, there was always added the example of the ashram which Mahatma Gandhi set up in the perspective of a spirituality of non-violence and a non-violent liberation. I visited the first ashram founded by Gandhi in South Africa where I met a part of the Gandhi family. In the center of the "house of prayer," as I see it, is the Gospel of peace. I also found receptivity to my suggestions among Protestant Christians and communities who were committed to peace.

Among the most beautiful and most enriching experiences of my life are the many years of cooperation with the Church of the Savior in Washington, DC. This is a strong group of ecumenically committed ministers and laity of various confessions. Their program is the Sermon on the Mount. Their spirituality is the Beatitudes. They are in many ways similar to the religious order of Taizé, but the majority are married. The entire family lives in spiritual-ity. Annually, from 1965 to 1979, I held a spiritual retreat for the core group in their own retreat house. I received much stimulation and encouragement from them. All their groups are schools of prayer. They live a powerful synthe-sis of contemplation and commitment to the cause of peace and justice. They are amazingly inventive in their concern for the poor and homeless. They are also politi-cally involved. In a word, they live a synthesis of faith and life. For me they are a hope-engendering image of the Christian Church toward which we all strive.

Also from the very beginning I have been in contact with the charismatic movement in the U.S.A. and beyond. I appreciate above all their positive attitude. Due to the spirit of praise they have grown in their capability to see the good first. Thus they shield themselves from the spirit of pessimism, bitterness, and fanaticism. The groups with which I have worked are completely ecumenically ori-ented. The same is also true of the charismatic groups in the Protestant churches. They prayerfully cultivate the spirit of community and Christian love of neighbor, espe-cially for the poor. They are, however, less politically in-volved than, for example, the Church of the Savior. I be-lieve, however, that one should not make that an accusation against them. Things must mature gradually. In addition, we dare not lose the vision of the differences of the gifts of grace.

I am also gratefully obliged to the members of the Focolari movement for their friendship and inspiration. They likewise embody an admirable synthesis of zeal and vision, prayer and neighborliness, Church and openness to the world.

As you look back on a long blessed life, for what are you now especially thankful to God?

When I see how through my efforts for the renewal of moral theology I have been allowed to liberate the conscience of many people from a legalism and moralism which produced a senseless scrupulosity and neurotic anxiety and compulsion which alienated many from the Church, I count it as a gift of God of which I am not worthy. Likewise, that I have been allowed to serve the maturing of genuine conscientiousness and respect for the conscience of others. It is a joy to me to see that many Christians are no longer plagued by the temptation Paul Claudel described: "Certainly, we love Christ, but nothing in the world will move us to love moralism." In union with many others who likewise think as I do and who have helped in the renewal of moral theology, I have been allowed to help many Christians so that they can now say from their hearts: "I love your law, O Lord."

My patron saint, Bernard of Clairvaux, wrote in his book *De consideratione* an admonition to the pope: "The laws of Justinian sound and crackle all day long in your palace." He admonished the pope to keep the hunters after honors and benefices at arm's length, to leave politics to others and to employ the time thus won to meditating on the Gospel and proclaiming it. He wished to "hear the law in which my heart rejoices" in the house of the pope and in the whole Church. That is also the desire of my life.

In all of these efforts I have received a great deal of help and encouragement from the houses of prayer and the communities in spiritual movements which I have described. During the depressing doctrinal trial, time and again I found refuge, new strength, and joy in the special houses of prayer, especially in Monroe, Michigan, with the IHM sisters who feel themselves particularly committed to the Alfonsian spirituality.

You have looked death in the eye many times. Do you have a fear of dying?

Yes, in my life I have had much to do with death. The death of my beloved parents hit me very hard. In late Fall, 1945, I returned from the Polish parish which had freed me from the Russian prisoner of war camp and perhaps even from death somewhere in Siberia or the Arctic Sea, to the golden anniversary of my parents—so I thought. Instead of that, I learned of the death of my mother. My first act was to go to the cemetery. My father understood wonderfully how to comfort me for he simply and soberly told me of the last hour of my mother's life: "I was sobbing and said to her, 'I have always prayed that I could die before you; for what am I without you?' In high German, like the pastor in his sermon, she said to me, 'Johannes, how can you cry? You know who decides on the hour of death for us, don't you?' " And my father added: "Then I promised your mother not to cry anymore." I would have been ashamed if then I had cried before him.

Two years later a telegram from my home reached me at Gars: "Father is preparing for death." I immediately set out. Nevertheless, I arrived home three hours after his death. What my brother and two sisters who were present at his death related to me was gripping. Father had the local pastor called as soon as he returned from the hospital in order to die at home. He got up, had himself shaved, put on his best feastday suit and received the sacrament of the dying sitting up. Then as he was once again in bed he said to my oldest brother: "Greet your brothers and sisters; for now the hour of my death has come. I am sorry that I cannot wait until they are all here." A few seconds later he was dead.

Gripping for me too was the death of my beloved teacher of New Testament exegesis, Father Brandhüber, who unstintingly encouraged and advised me during the writing of my work *The Law of Christ*. He was also my father confessor. A half-year before his death he said to me: "If God grants me one more year then I will complete the two important works on the Christology of the great Syrian theologians." It came out differently. Lung cancer destroyed him while he was still hoping to be able to complete his life work. I gently tried to turn him away from this idea. Since as a former medic I could deal with the sick, I took over the night watch by his death-bed. Every two hours I had to change his shirt, because he was sweating so profusely. As I changed him once more, he motioned to me to come closer to his bed. He said to me: "I have now understood: I desire to be released so as to be with Christ. What do my manuscripts mean to me now?" From that hour on his sweating ceased. A wonderful calm came over his face until the moment of death.

The first time I felt very close to death was in 1942 at the battle around Kursk. Blood flowed heavily from my head wound. My five stretcher-bearers were already all hit before me, two of them fatally. My attempt to bind up my head wound myself would not stop the bleeding. I awaited death as a release from this valley of tears. Nevertheless, I came out of it with my life intact.

In 1977 while facing a five-hour-long operation on my throat, which, as I knew, entailed a great risk, I fell into a deep sleep shortly before the nurse came to give me my first injection. During this sleep I had an extremely vivid dream. In a very beautiful valley I saw the Good Shepherd, who motioned to me. I woke up full of happiness. The young nurse who had just come in was totally perplexed. She said: "Now I am going to do what I should not do. But I simply must ask you. How can you in the face of such a grim operation be so happy? The fact that you are a priest does not explain that. Many times I have seen priests in similar situations full of unrest, exactly like everyone else." Since I was mute, I wrote on my slate: "It is an undeserved gift of God. Were I not constantly thankful, it would be lost." I had interpreted my dream, thinking of the burdensome doctrinal trial, thus: "Now you may leave this valley of tears." After I had my tranquilizing injection I had another dream. I ran from one counter to another trying to buy a train ticket. But everywhere I was told, "There is no train ticket here for you." That meant then, I still had to stay in this valley of tears.

Then in 1980 as I was awaiting an extremely risky six-hour operation I again had a consoling dream. It appeared as if God was assuring me. "Do not worry about your friends. All will see my face." Again, the nurse was astonished. I would have died happy. Nevertheless, I am thankful for every day which the Lord has added to my life.

I will attempt to respond concretely to your question about whether or not I fear dying. It can well be that a fear of death will yet overtake me, exactly as it does others. However, did Jesus not suffer the fear of death for us all? I view my death and everything which will immediately follow with trust, and that despite all the sins which I have committed during my long life. I have oriented my life in view of my death to the program of the Sermon on the Mount: "Blessed are the merciful, for they shall receive mercy." I attempt to forgive from my heart all those who have injured me. And likewise as a moral theologian and pastor, I place everything on the card of mercy that I also might expect everything from the mercy of God.

* * * * * * * * * *

Shortly before Easter of that year [1989] my friend Dr. Licheri came to me in Gars, where I have been in retirement since April, 1988. He asked me a couple more questions which refer to the events after the congress of moral theologians at the Lateran in November, 1988.

After the death of the beloved Pope John Paul I, some were afraid that the next pope could be Cardinal Siri. You dared to predict firmly and confidently: "The next pope will be called John Paul II and it will be no other than Karol Woityla." What do you think now, after almost eleven years and the recent stormy events of this pontificate?

After the election of Karol Woityla I was very happy, not only because of my feeling of gratitude to the Polish people, but also because, due to our work together during the Council, I had an appreciation of Karol Woityla. I knew his genial gift, among others, for languages. He is gregarious in the best sense of the word, unconventional, devout, full of apostolic zeal.

In the subsequent years of his pontificate he has shown a radiant power, has courageously involved himself for the concerns of the third world, has made many prophetic gestures, as for example, the visit to the synagogue in Rome, the Lutheran Church in Rome, the humble meeting with the head of the Anglican Church community in Canterbury and, not least, the day of peace in Assisi with the representatives of the great religions of the world. It would be an act of ingratitude even to God to view that as an everyday experience or even to overlook it.

In regard to what I believe is his rigid interpretation of *Humanae vitae* and sexual morality in general, I refer to the doctrinal trial launched against me. From that it will be undoubtedly clear that Karol Woityla did not bring this strictness to the Vatican. It was in any case, as I came to experience directly, the official line of the Doctrinal Congregation. Justice to the pope obliges me to point this out. This was also one of the many-leveled reasons why I am publishing this volume. My best friends in the Vatican repeatedly assured me: "The pope himself is more open-minded than his immediate advisors."

Nevertheless, the events around the Congress of Moralists organized by Msgr. Carlo Caffarra and the "Opus Dei" have disturbed me deeply. In the text and the tone of the papal address of November 12, 1988, I no longer recognized the Karol Woityla whom I knew and respected. Like many others, I was shocked and at first speechless. Numerous telephone calls, letters, meetings with religion teachers, priests and pastoral assistants have aroused me out of my silence.

Thus, with a heavy heart I decided on December 1, 1988 to write personally to the pope in order to inform him of my view of the alarming situation of the Church in the German-speaking lands. However, when after six weeks I still did not receive confirmation of its having been received, I published my essay "For a Renewed Trust in the Church," simultaneously in the magazines *Christ in der Gegenwart* and *Il Regno* (Bologna). It was an appeal to the pope and to the whole Church to verify whether the severe interpretation as it was proclaimed in the papal address before the Congress of Moralists in November is received in the Church, or whether more opened-hearted interpretation of the great episcopacies like that of the German-speaking lands and the French bishops makes *Humanae vitae* more receivable. A question of reception plays a great role in the declaration of the papal and episcopal Magisterium, as indeed is well known. I want to point this out clearly.

Ultimately I also signed the "Cologne Declaration Against Resignation in the Church." Had I received an encouraging word from the pope, I certainly would have done everything in my power to dissuade my colleagues from a public declaration. They could, indeed, also have sent it directly to the pope himself. It would have been, in my opinion, better if a timely direct dialogue with the pope could have taken place.

What were the reactions to your manifold statements about this renewed flourishing of an anxiety-provoking sexual rigorism?

I received hundreds of telephone calls and letters. About five percent were curses and insults. Another five percent promised prayers for my conversion, or believed to know that God in his foreknowledge of this sin of mine had already punished me with cancer. About ninety percent expressed their gratitude. Astonishingly many spoke of how they themselves, their grown children or acquaintances had been deterred by my statement from carrying out their intentions to leave the Church. I believe that these reactions give us a rather accurate snapshot of all of us "beloved little animals" in the ark of Noah. I console myself and others with the following parable: One day Noah complained bitterly to God about the strange and burdensome animals that he brought with him on the ark. God answered smiling: "But my dear friend Noah, do not

forget that you are also one of these beloved little
animals."

What was the reaction of the Vatican?

Until January 30, 1989, I heard nothing from the Vatican. That was the day on which the Catholic news service
(KNA) came to Gars for an interview and asked me precisely: "Why did you and your colleagues not turn directly
to the pope instead of alarming the public?" My response
was twofold. First of all, the public, committed Catholics
and above all teachers of religion and pastors, were the
ones who alarmed and concerned us. Secondly, already on
December 1, I had written to the pope by express mail and
still have received no confirmation that the letter was received. I gave the KNA the text of my letter to the pope
with the firm hope that the KNA would understand how to
bring this letter to the attention of the pope. On February
7, an Assessor of the Secretary of State of the Vatican sent
me a friendly letter with the assurance that the pope had
taken notice of my letter. The tone was completely
friendly, and of course also contained a reference to the
public statement which could make the dialogue more difficult. Unfortunately I have not been informed as to when
the pope really received my letter.

On February 16, on the front page of the *Osservatore
Romano,* an unsigned essay appeared. It fundamentally repeated the validity and obligation of the prohibition of
artificial contraception without exception, but did not repeat any of the anxiety-generating expressions of the address to the Congress of Moralists. The decisive thing is
that a pastoral understanding for those married people
who turn to artificial contraception in cases of necessity

was expressly called for. This for me is a decisive outcome, even if not satisfactory in all respects.

Hard questions press upon us moral theologians and all who have to do with pastoral activity. We experience pangs of conscience when Church authority demands from us an uncritical teaching that the prohibition of every kind of artificial contraception without exception is a demand of the natural moral law when neither the Magisterium nor we can provide convincing reasons for this position. For according to the Catholic tradition and the understanding of all ethicists the demands of the natural moral law are capable of being grounded in argument from communicable experience and reflection. Thank God it is now no longer openly maintained that it is strengthened by divine revelation. For if we had to teach that, we would have had fear in our soul to call upon the name of God in vain.

How can we make clear to men and women that the command of the decalogue not to kill allows no exception as long as the papal Magisterium holds fast to the theory of a "just war" and justifies mass killing in a war that is considered just (a shift to a non-violent defense would better correspond to the biblical revelation), while at the same time it is supposed to be stressed that contraception under all thinkable circumstances is objectively disallowed!

We experience incomparable fear in our soul if we should obediently "proclaim" the objective validity of the prohibition of contraception even where this would endanger the peace or even the continued existence of a marriage. Or are we, according to the essay in the *Osservatore Romano*, to say simply in such cases that the married people should follow their consciences? It seems to me that such an interpretation is necessary if we are to act with pastoral sensitivity. With that, however, a key sentence in the statements of many bishops' conferences on *Humanae vitae* is again affirmed.

Because no confirmation of the reception had arrived by January 30, 1989, I gave the text of my letter to the pope to the KNA. Likewise, the readers of this book also have a right to see its text.

(Document 17)
Letter to Pope John Paul II
               Gars am Inn, December 1, 1988

Dear Father in Christ,

We have many reasons for loving you, not just because of your high office but also because of your untiring enthusiasm for justice and peace, because of your closeness to those in need, and for many other reasons.

Love for your person, high esteem for your office and the responsibility we all share for handing on the faith to the critically-minded generation of today and to those who will come after us nevertheless compel me to express openly my reservations about what I regard as your over-emphasis on too rigorously interpreted norms in the field of sexual ethics.

Naturally like you we are aware of our duty to do what we can so that Christians may love and foster chastity. But it is precisely in this field that the saying applies: "The bow is broken when drawn too tight." If in this difficult field we demand even an iota more than we can reasonably justify from revelation or from reason inspired by faith, we lose credibility. Quite simply, we are no longer listened to.

I was shattered to read recently that among 6,000 readers of *Weltbild*, a journal that is very loyal and devoted to the Pope (Nos. 23 and 24, November 4, 28, 1988), only 12% of the faithful under 50 and only 25% of those over 50 are ready to listen to the present papal teaching on questions of sexual morality, while in general the same people are fully prepared to value papal authority very highly on questions of faith and morals. Similar findings have resulted from surveys in other parts of the world.

Recently I had occasion to listen to a large group of highly-qualified teachers of religion, men and women loyal to the Church, telling me how difficult it has been and still is for them to calm the waves caused by your address to moral theologians on November 12, 1988.

The heading in *L'Osservatore Romano* of November 13, 1988, is something one can and must agree with: "One cannot speak of a painstaking search for the truth if one does not take into account what the Magisterium teaches." But if this Magisterium of the Church becomes the battle-cry of intransigent people who boast about standing particularly close to the Pope, and if it becomes a weapon against those who resist far too strict an interpretation only on secondary points, then one does not serve well the Church, its mission or even the Petrine ministry.

I have before me the text of the lecture "Who is like the Lord our God?" given by Professor Msgr. Carlo Caffarra to the Congress of Moralists, to which you paid particular honor by receiving and addressing its participants. The level of scholarship is far below what is needed. It seems to call radically into question any attempt to justify or analyze moral norms on teleological grounds. On page 7 of the typescript we find: "That is why once man has raised himself to the ethical level he is no longer interested in detail or ultimately in the historical possibilities, consequences and results of his action: he is raised above such calculation."

The first thing that has to be noted against a naive and indeed alarming misinterpretation of the teleological approach is that what is involved is in no way a calculation of utility, but a careful weighing of the consequences with regard to healthy and healing relationships, with regard to bearing fruit in love and peace in a context of solidarity.

Caffarra's statement occurs in a context in which he uses very abstract ideas that are remote from life and unproved assertions concerning tradition in an effort to prove that the norm laid down by *Humanae vitae* (the ban on artificial birth control) does not admit of an exception in any case.

Along with virtually the entire tradition of the Eastern Churches and a large part of the Roman Catholic tradition, St. Alphonsus Liguori taught that even in questions of the natural law there is room for *epikeia* (*Theologia moralis* 1: I:tr. II, c. IV, n. 201). By this he does not of course mean the highest norms of the commandment to love God and neighbor that is inscribed in our hearts. Nevertheless, he applies the possibility of *epikeia* explicitly to *coitus interruptus*—which at that time was the only non-magical method of birth control—and the cooperation of the wife who knows her husband is going to use this method. Like the other moral theologians of that time he too teaches that *coitus interruptus* in itself contradicts the procreative sense of the marriage act and is therefore to be rejected. Still, he explicitly mentions cases in which couples have good reason to want the marriage act not to lead to conception. He too saw a high value in abstinence, but left open the possibility of *epikeia* for a just cause (*justa ex causa*).

In his lecture to the Congress of Moralists, as in earlier statements, Carlo Caffarra does not distinguish whether in an actual situation procreation would be desirable or whether it would be irresponsible. As an example let us take the kind of case that I have repeatedly been faced with: because a woman has already given birth to children with genetic defects, she suffers from a pregnancy psychosis. Gynecologists and psychiatrists are convinced that the woman can once again become capable of living a married life and can be restored to her family to help bring up her handicapped children if through a combination of sterilization and psychotherapy she can be freed from her psychotic fear. The strict moral theologian says "No," on the ground that the woman's reproductive organs are not diseased. In other cases that occur not infrequently, the rigorous insistence on the Church's norms brings a marriage to the breaking-point. In the actual case "natural family planning" is not applicable. The husband is alienated from his wife through her

obedience to the Church and also from the
Church in anger at its rigorism. In such cases is it
evident that all artificial methods of birth control
are absolutely immoral when what is ultimately
involved is maintaining the mutual self-giving of
marriage and the bond of loyalty?

According to Caffarra, whatever the situation may be, what is involved is nothing less than
"an attack on God's holiness" and the pride of
wanting to be "like God," and further similar no-
tions. How can one argue so simplistically? That
is not the image of God which Jesus makes tangible and visible for us.

In your papal address to the participants in
the Congress, who were presented to you by
Msgr. Caffarra, we find: "This moral norm does
not allow of any exceptions: no personal or social
circumstance has ever been, is, or ever will be,
able to make such an act rightly ordered." As far
as I am concerned it is beyond question that there
are moral prohibitions which do not admit of any
exception. For example, torture can never ever
be morally justified, especially when it is used to
extort statements and confessions. Pius XII stated
that with great sorrow about an extremely inglo-
rious earlier Church tradition and the doctrinal
statements of popes that supported it. Similarly it
is immediately obvious that rape and similar acts
always offend against the moral law.

But does this also apply to the norm that
every marriage act must be open to generation?
To put it another way, are artificial means of controlling conception worthy of condemnation in
all circumstances? The majority of moral theolo-

gians side with St. Thomas Aquinas in teaching that the more complex and more remote from the supreme principle of love a derived moral norm is, the smaller is its degree of certainty and the less it excludes the application of *epikeia*.

In the Augustinian tradition the norm of the actual openness of sexual intercourse to procreation was an absolute norm—because of his pessimism with regard to sexuality. For him and his followers the sexual act counted as something degrading and shameful, and thus needed to be excused and made moral (*excusatio, cohonestatio*) by the direct intention of procreation. But today one can no longer appeal to this tradition. Rather, it should make us careful about what we say.

How can one expect the critically-minded people of today, including devout Christians, to accept the statement that in the interpretation of the norm laid down by *Humanae vitae* every exception (all *epikeia*) must be absolutely excluded, and then put forward the statement: "In reality what is called into question by the rejection of this teaching is the very idea of the holiness of God" ("A ben guardare ciò che è messo in questione, rifiutando quell'insegnamento, è l'idea stessa della Santità di Dio"—papal address of November 12, 1988)?

Furthermore, we are shaken to have to face the question whether one can really say of the norm of *Humanae vitae* when interpreted so strictly that "it has been inscribed by the creative hand of God and has been confirmed by him in revelation" ("essa e stata inscritta dalla mano creatice de Dio ed è stata da Lui confermata nella

Rivelazione"). Where can such a confirmation be found? If indeed we consider how many good and intelligent Christians inside and outside the Catholic Church simply cannot join in deducing such a rigorous interpretation, and how they find scandalous, indeed offensive, the thought-models, methods of argument and imputations of guilt proposed by Carlo Caffarra and others, then one should not teach in so undifferentiated and simplistic a way: "To call it into question is thus equivalent to refusing to God himself the obedience of our intelligence" ("Metterla in discussione, pertanto, equivale a rifiutare a Dio stesso l'obbedienza della nostra intelligenza"—the same papal address of November 12, 1988).

Immense questions concerning the history of the exercise of the Magisterium by the popes are thrown into question by the following stricture against any analysis of statements of this kind: "Because the Church's Magisterium has been instituted to enlighten the conscience, any appeal to this conscience in order to contest the truth of what has been taught by the Magisterium involves the rejection of the Catholic concept of th the Magisterium and of the moral con- nce" ("Poichè il Magistero della Chiesa é instituito per illuminare la coscienza, richia- questa coscienza di contestare la verità di insegnato dal Magistero comporta il ri- a concezione cattolica sia del Magis- coscienza morale"—from the same

ally-minded person, and indeed evout Christian who is devoted

and loyal to the Church and to the successor of
Peter, needs to subject such a statement to historical analysis and questioning, perhaps by trying to
put this question: "Has anyone who, by appeal-
ing to conscience, subjected to analysis and question the teaching of Boniface VIII and several of
his successors about the plenary powers of the
pope over all secular realms and spheres, thereby
rejected at least by implication the Catholic concept of both the Magisterium and conscience?"

If only one particular theological tendency is
accepted in the Vatican, and indeed with such
severity as in the case of the Congress of Moralists organized by Carlo Caffarra, then for all of us
numerous and painful questions are raised.

On the other hand, the more collegially the
Petrine ministry is able to encourage the diver-
sity of cultures and traditions and the quest of the
different theological cultures, the greater will be
the trust the Petrine Magisterium instills in us all.
For if the pope is directly drawn into intransigent
interpretations and the most shocking kinds of argumentation, then we are all plunged into a crisis
and are compelled by our loyalty to the Church
to express our distress and agony.

The shocking nature of the present crisis is
demonstrated above all in the field of papal
teaching on sexual morality, to which people
react most sensitively. But, in my view, much
more serious is the danger that as a consequence
of the present intensification of polarization, if
the pope himself is primarily involved in his own
person, then the Magisterium of the pope and the
bishops can ultimately no longer develop its full

potential even on quite central questions of our faith. And yet the present generation's need for faith is already so great!

Dear Father in Christ,

I am an old man who already has more than one foot in the grave. I love my Church passionately and I also love the successor of Peter. And to my eyes there are many reasons that make him worth loving. In order to be able to await God's mercy with confidence in the hour of death, I have throughout my life been concerned to follow a compassionate and merciful moral theology and pastoral practice. Married couples in their distress must be made to feel the balm of compassionate love. In thousands of letters and in hearing thousands of confessions I have learned the extent to which good Christians are grievously hurt by rigorism in sexual matters.

Harsh formulations, such as those favored by Carlo Caffarra and his allies, hurt people and re-open old wounds. They make the ministry of healing and saving love more difficult for all of us. If, for example, we hear Carlo Caffarra say triumphantly that at the ethical level one does not need to bother in any way with foreseeable consequences, then we can only weep and pray when we are asked what we have to say to that.

These and other considerations have compelled me to pour my heart out to you. If you should feel yourself injured by what I have said, I ask your pardon.

"The pope's Magisterium" (*Magistero del Papa*), a phrase now so often used, should not become a battle-cry of the Church's intransigent honor-seekers and as a result become for many others an incomprehensible myth.

Thus I remain in the love of the most sacred heart of Jesus,

Your devoted servant,
Bernhard Häring

[This translation is from *The Tablet*, June 30, 1990.]

In view of this situation we wish to pray:

God, our Father, without you we can do nothing which will bring us all to wholeness. Pour your spirit out over us so that together in love we will search for the truth, so that we will take not a single iota away from your holy will, but also will not pile a single unnecessary burden on others or ourselves. Help us so to interpret your holy law of love and justice that all women and men of good will can understand the word of your son become human: "My yoke is gentle, my burden is light."

Grant that in disputes we not injure love. Help us to be thankful for the Petrine service in the Church, even when we, like your apostle Paul, raise serious doubts. Grant all of us in the Church a mutual trust, without flattery, in the spirit of freedom and candor and in absolute honesty.

This we ask through Christ, our Lord.

9

IN RETROSPECT:
MY EXPERIENCE WITH
THE CHURCH

---

*In closing I would like to pose a question which will
draw things together. Looking back now, how do you see
your experience with the Church and your work in and for
the Church? Which predominates: The positive or the
negative?*

Were I to identify the Church with the tradition from
the Roman Inquisition to the Doctrinal Congregation as I
have experienced both with others and also for myself, I
would say that the balance for me is rather negative. I can
understand why people who fix their view only on this
institution leave the Church out of disillusionment. However, such a fixation contradicts our faith.

I see the Church embodied and presented in exemplary Christian families as I have experienced it in my parents' house and in many other places. There the Church is
tangible. In Russia during the Stalin period I experienced
the Church in families and in neighborhood circles who
had held on to their faith and their lively trust in God
throughout a long period without priests. Reason enough

for joy! I have experienced the Church intensely in my religious order. It was and is for me a homeland of faith, a model of the Pilgrim Church. Of course there were also tensions between those who joyfully greeted and went along with the exegetical, theological and then the conciliar renewal, and the others who anxiously asked themselves whether this was the Church, the theology, the religious life that for so long were their home. At the same time, through a patient dialogue, these tensions have turned out to be largely fruitful.

I experienced the Church time and again in the saints through the reading of their lives which bore such a strong witness. Still more I have known the Church in encounters with the small unpretentious believers of our time as well as with imposing prophetic figures.

After a partially depressing experience in the preconciliar period, above all in the commission which was dominated by the Holy Office, there was for many, and also for me, the extraordinary experience of the breakthrough in the Council. In this the papacy reached a high point, precisely in the experience of collegiality. The Church has experienced in this century great popes. Pope John Paul I inscribed himself deeply in the hearts of the faithful in thirty days with his precious, winning smile.

Today many negatively loaded associations are attached to the word "Vatican." I think that I am able to say that with me the positive experiences very much dominate. When Pope John XXIII was asked how many people worked in the Vatican, he is supposed to have answered: "Probably about half." I believe that there is much work done in the Vatican, ungrudgingly so, perhaps too much by some. Much more could be left to the local churches. As an academic teacher in Rome I feel that I owe a great debt of gratitude to the Congregation of Studies. Under the leadership of Cardinal Garonne and Cardinal Schröffer, this part of the Vatican was for me a model reflection of the Council breakthrough. Theological research was encouraged. I look with awe at the patient, courageous work of the Secretariat for Christian Unity. Here also one could draw up a long list of clear rays of hope.

I have thankfully experienced the Church in many dozens of general chapters of religious orders of men and women who invited me to collaborate or to preach a retreat. How much drive and enthusiasm and how much patient work could one experience there! Since 1966, above all in North America, I have been calling for a renewal in the life of prayer as the center of the post-conciliar renewal. As my model for this I have taken "houses of prayer," places where the integration of faith and life, where worship "in spirit and in truth," could take place. I can only look with astonishment at the many creative initiatives and the persevering elan related to them.

From the beginning I have also been in close contact with the charismatic renewal, which was a response to the theological efforts for a stronger emphasis on pneumatology (study of the Spirit). In the critical years around 1968 I met many groups which, through the spirit of praise, were and are immune to destructive criticism. I also had contact with the Focolari movement which binds together devotion with working for one's neighbor and community.

In the theological summer courses which I gave during the long academic holidays in Africa, Asia, Latin America and North America and also in various European countries, we experienced together the Church, the Pilgrim Church on the way to a deeper self-understanding, in the search for a praying theology.

Time and again in Africa I gratefully experienced

MY EXPERIENCE WITH THE CHURCH

what a living liturgy can be, a joy in God and a joy in community. The numerous catechists and their families whom I met in many countries in Africa impressed me deeply. They remind me of the reports in the Acts of the Apostles of the first generation of deacons. Here is a new form of "cleric" without clericalism.

I experienced Church in the base communities of Africa, the Philippines and Brazil. It is the "Church from below," the humble, saving-historical Church, the all-embracing "People of God" Church which gives hope for the future.

I experienced Church in an especially joyful way with my students at the Academia Alfonsiana, at the Gregorian University, and at numerous ecumenical faculties. How much love and enthusiasm is spread there!

I experienced Church as an ecumenical hope in the more than one dozen retreats that I was permitted to hold for Protestant pastors and their wives. What a power of faith! What patient hope and what a persevering effort for the heart's desire of Jesus, "that all may be one"!

In fact, I have experienced so much love and encouragement everywhere that the "condiments" supplied by the Holy Office can perhaps be viewed as something like "salt and pepper" which provide the spice to life and ward off mold.

I love the Church because Christ loved it, loved it to the utmost extreme. I love it even where I discover painful attitudes and structures which I do not find in harmony with the Gospel. I love it as it is because Christ also loved me with all my imperfections, with all my shadows and constantly gives me the first fruits of his Kingdom so that my life may correspond to his eternal plan.

I experience the Church in the celebration of the eucharist. Christ and the Church with him remind me of all the limitless evidence of love, grace and mercy. In this the Church helps me to form a grateful memory. If we open ourselves to this and gratefully remember all the good which has flowed to us in the Church and constantly flows to us, then we can and will all succeed in giving even the suffering from the Church its place in the heart of Jesus.